Leisure Walks near Dublin

Leisure Walks near Dublin

Joss Lynam

Gill Books

Gill Books
Hume Avenue, Park West, Dublin 12
www.gillbooks.ie

Gill Books is an imprint of M.H. Gill & Co.

© Joss Lynam 2004
978 0 7171 3562 2
Maps by EastWest Mapping
Design by XO Design
Print origination by Carole Lynch
Printed in Ireland

The paper used in this book comes from the wood pulp of managed forests. For every tree felled, at least one tree is planted, thereby renewing natural resources.

A CIP catalogue record for this book is available from the British Library.

The maps in this book are reproduced from
Ordnance Survey Ireland Permit No. 7779
© Ordnance Survey Ireland and Government of Ireland

10 9 8 7

Important Note

Every effort has been made to ensure that the text and maps in this guidebook are correct at time of publication but neither the author nor the publishers accept any responsibility for errors or omissions.
Furthermore, changes will inevitably take place that will render portions of this guidebook outdated and incorrect. If errors are found the publishers will be very pleased to hear of them.

Contents

Thanks

My thanks are due to many organisations and people who helped me to write this book, both wittingly and unwittingly.

Most importantly my thanks to Coillte, the Wicklow Mountains National Park and all other landowners who permit walkers on their property.

This book could not have been written until the Ordnance Survey Ireland published the Discovery Series 1:50,000 scale maps. The old 'half-inch' maps by reason of their small scale could not possibly have included the amount of detail that is needed for these short walks. I have been known to grunt about small errors but that does not negate the huge debt that all walkers owe to the OSI for the rapid and generally efficient publication of this series.

For maps also, I am greatly indebted to all the orienteers who have mapped the orienteering areas of Dublin and Wicklow. These very detailed maps on scales of 1:10,000 and 1:15,000 have been invaluable on many walks, especially in the woods, where the OSI maps, not just because of their smaller scale, but because their cartographical method (aerial survey), cannot pick out the small paths which delight walkers. Perhaps a dozen times I have rummaged in the box that contains the crumpled maps of my orienteering experiences over nearly thirty years to find the one which will help me.

My thanks to Barry Dalby of EastWest Mapping for his work on the maps. It was a bit of a wrench to switch from hand-drawn to computer-drawn sketch maps, but the change had to be made and I knew that I couldn't have a better cartographer, both for his experience in the work and his knowledge of my requirements.

I would like to thank the companions who came with me on many of these walks — Liam Convery, Tommy Ellis, Bill Hannon, my daughter Ruth and son-in-law Don. Sometimes it was just for company, but often so that I could take advantage of their local knowledge. Either way I was able to add the pleasure of good company to the excitement of exploration of new walks.

In Gill & Macmillan it was, as ever, a great pleasure to work with Fergal Tobin who puts up patiently with all my foibles, and who is actually personally responsible for one walk (guess which!) in this book. My respect and thanks yet again to D Rennison Kunz for her patient coping with all problems; it was good (though not unexpected) to find that she is still the glue which holds G & M together.

My wife ... I can only repeat my gratitude for her support, and wonder (as my friends do) at her tolerance of my sins. Nora joined me on some walks, made valuable suggestions, read every description, pointed out the discrepancies, queried the uncertainties, was not afraid to argue (and win) her point. This is on top of feeding me, providing tea at all hours, putting up with my working on this book until 11 p.m. at night, driving a second car when needed, and in general, being tolerant far beyond the call of marital love. Tolerance nearly broke down over my last book and I was told quite clearly, that if I ever had New Year's Day as a deadline again, it would be grounds for divorce. So this time I staggered back up to the office after my birthday party to meet the deadline.

Introduction

I am now in my eightieth year and each year my limbs complain more strongly about the misuse they have received for the last sixty years on mountains all over the world. So some years ago they welcomed the proposal from Fergal Tobin to write a guidebook about walks round Dublin — easy walks, short walks — not exceeding three hours in duration. It was a new experience for me — I started looking at walks I'd never even considered doing before, and I provided him with one book of forty easy walks some five years ago. I enjoyed finding these walks and writing about them so much that here are another thirty-five of the same. Like the last collection (*Easy Walks near Dublin*) none is longer than three hours, they are mostly within an hour's drive of Dublin and all within my now even-more-limited capabilities.

Preparing this second collection has been of greater interest than the first since I had already picked out most of my old favourites and had to do further research for new walks, which involved pestering friends and relations for ideas. Once again I have to apologise to Northsiders for the paucity of walks north of the Liffey, but this time I have at least explored their beaches. Apart from my possible territorial bias and my inherent bias in favour of the hills, it has been difficult to find walks north and west of Dublin — there simply is not the terrain where we can walk freely. South of Dublin and into Wicklow we are fortunate in having plenty of forests owned by Coillte, the Irish Forestry Board, who permit walking in all their forests. Many of the hill walks which I have included are only possible because access through Coillte enables the walker to get onto the open hillside without crossing pastures and cultivated fields. Of course, what I describe as a fine area of mature trees may be a battlefield of piled branches and rutted extraction tracks when *you* get to walk there in a couple years. Because of felling I have already had to change one description I wrote a year ago when I started prospecting. Fortunately Coillte are conserving some areas of deciduous trees; these make and will continue to make splendid walks.

This book has several aims. Firstly, I hope it will help Dublin people (and others) who are not walkers to start that activity. Secondly, most of these walks are suitable for families and for people who for whatever reason do not want full-day walks. Finally, I hope this book may stimulate people like myself, whose best walking days are over, to keep active, and even if they hang up their boots, at least to keep going in trainers! The first two categories may not be committed walkers and may not be expert map-readers so I have tried to be almost pedantic in my descriptions of how to follow each walk. A walk in the countryside is not just about exercising the legs; you can get that by walking round the block ten times. I want you to enjoy the environment and so wherever possible I have tried to inject some 'personality' on each walk with history, natural history and even personal experiences.

I have also tried wherever possible to choose walks which are circular and those which can be reached by public transport. The latter have the advantage that they are often less dependent on circularity. I have used the term 'car' for private transport, but a bicycle will go wherever a car will, and often a bit further. Two cars can often be replaced by one car and a bicycle!

I hope that this book will also be useful to visitors from the rest of Ireland and from abroad. There are many, surely, who are not serious walkers but would enjoy a short walk or two and, as strangers, may appreciate the detail I have given here.

A few Dos and Don'ts — mainly for the hill walks

- Always carry some food and (more important) drink
- Always plan to be back before dark
- Do carry a torch in winter
- Do carry a simple first aid box
- Do tell someone where you've gone
- Don't be afraid to turn back if you are tired or the weather turns bad
- Don't walk solo except on frequented paths
- Do check the weather forecast before starting

Access

At the time of writing there are no problems of access on any of these walks — nor are there at all likely to be in the future. They are on private property *only* on the open hillside. In the *most* unlikely event of meeting a 'private' sign, please comply — these walks are mostly *not* rights-of-way. If you ever do meet a problem, please inform me! In general, access in Wicklow isn't a problem. This is the result of having a body — the Wicklow Uplands Council — on which farmers, recreational users, and community and local tourism bodies are represented and any difficulties that arise can be settled amicably.

There may, of course, be diversions, especially in the forests, if work is in progress.

I have not knowingly routed any of these walks across private property, except — and this is quite a big exception — on the unfenced mountains, to which traditionally there has been no objection to access. But (outside of the Wicklow Mountains National Park) the mountains are all private property; even commonage is private property, though there may be dozens of farmers sharing it. Without access to these hills our walking would be terribly restricted so, if only for selfish reasons (and I hope for other reasons too), we must respect that private property, realising that the mountains are an important part of the farming industry — yes it's an industry now — which we must do nothing to damage. Chiefly that means not frightening sheep and that means NO DOGS. Dogs are man's best friend — but the sheep's worst enemy. Look at it from your dog's point of view: a farmer is legally entitled to shoot any dog he sees annoying sheep; very few farmers enjoy shooting dogs, but sometimes they have to do it. Why put your dog at risk?

Please don't take a dog on the following walks (birds and other wildlife, sheep, regulations):
Numbers 4, 6, 11, 12, 14, 15, 16, 17, 18, 19, 20, 22, 23, 25, 29, 30, 32, 35.
You may see other dogwalkers, but that doesn't make it right!

I can add in 2003 that I do see some progress. There have been some high profile cases of 'active' refusal of farmers to allow access, but there is a growing understanding in tourism, in government circles and amongst farmers that some form of agreement has to be reached so that walkers can go most places that they want to, and that farmers will be protected against claims and damage. I do not think legislation is the answer — there is growing dissatisfaction in England with the actual results of the 'Right to Roam' legislation — and I think the most positive approach in Ireland will be the creation of further partnerships like the Wicklow Uplands Council and the Mournes Heritage Trust. The increasing support for payment to farmers for maintenance of paths is also helpful.

A final word for walking anywhere in Ireland, not just on these thirty-five walks. Wherever you walk, except on the public road, you are not there by right, but at the discretion of the landowner and if for any reason you are asked to leave, do so graciously. But if there is some doubt, a polite request for permission will usually bring assent.

If you are already an experienced walker, you can ignore the next heading!

Maps and Navigation

The minimum that anyone who uses this book needs is some kind of a road map in order to find the walks. You may already have a road map, but if you haven't I suggest the OSI 1:250,000 (¼ inch to 1 mile) map 'East', because it will also help you to pick out the mountains mentioned in summit views. The sketch maps which accompany each walk are all you need, with the text, to guide you round many of the walks, particularly the low-level ones, but when tackling the longer walks on the hills, I do suggest that the OSI Discovery 1:50,000 (1¼ inches to 1 mile) maps are worth carrying. They are not difficult to read, they can obviously tell you a lot more about your surroundings than the small sketch maps can, and are very useful if by chance you stray from the route. The cost is not high — two Discovery Sheets (50 and 56) cover ninety per cent of the walks. To preserve your map (and this guidebook!) carry them in a plastic bag, or a map case slung round your neck.

Recently two larger scale maps have been published. The Wicklow Mountains National Park map at 1:30,000 published by Harvey Maps in Scotland covers many of the walks, and its larger scale enables it to carry more detail than the Discovery series. The map of Glendalough and Glenmalur (Glenmalure) at 1:25,000 published by Pat Healy is also very useful for that area. I have noted them, where appropriate, for walks.

On some of the mountain walks where you might run into mist, I have suggested you carry a compass, but even on these walks no accurate compass work is involved. I hope, however, that, when you have worked through a selection of walks in this book, some of you may be tempted to bigger things, and that you will progress to being able to find your way in safety on the hills, woods and watersides of Ireland.

I have used the metric system for heights and distances because all our modern maps are metric, even our road signs are gradually going metric.

Timing

I have taken the risk of suggesting how long a walk might take you, so I had better explain my method. Many years ago Naismith, a Scottish mountaineer, worked out a rule of thumb based on distance covered plus height gained. For my variant of 'Naismith's Rule', I am assuming that you can cover a kilometre in somewhere between fifteen and twenty minutes on the flat, depending on the surface on which you are walking and that every 100 m of height gained will take an extra fifteen minutes. So a walk of 6 km with a climb of 200 m will take ninety minutes for the flat walk plus thirty minutes for the ascent — total two hours. If the going was very rough on half the walk I would add an extra quarter-hour. I would not, however, like to claim complete consistency. Time yourself on a couple of walks to find out whether you are faster or slower than the times I give, and plan accordingly. Please remember that the times given do not allow for any rests or stops of more than a couple of minutes. Especially in the winter when the days are short, it is important to make sure that you can finish your planned walk well before dark, allowing for likely stops and delays.

Clothing and Equipment

I have given some suggestions on equipment with each walk. Everybody owns trainers (or walking shoes) and for many walks either are perfectly adequate. Boots are recommended if the going is very rough, muddy or boggy — wet feet are unpleasant, especially in winter.

One of the advantages of the Irish climate is its changeability; if it's raining now, it may be fine soon. But the converse is equally true so it is generally unwise to go walking without protection against rain. Most of us possess a light anorak — that will suffice on many walks, as mostly will a plastic mac. If I think greater protection is required — against strong winds and low temperatures — I mention 'weather gear', by which I mean a 'fleece' or extra sweater, and perhaps a woolly cap and gloves as well as windproof rain gear. As you go higher it gets colder, wetter and windier. On the summits of the bigger mountains in this book, such as Silsean (Walk 22) or Church Mountain (Walk 23), it is 4°–6° Celsius colder than at sea level, the wind is nearly twice as strong, and the annual rainfall is more than double that in Dublin. So be sure that you are well-prepared on such walks. On the other hand if you choose a warm summer day with a good forecast for your walk, then such precautions can be considerably scaled down.

Walking sticks. My arthritic knees remind me whenever I walk downhill that I should have taken to using a pair of walking sticks long before I did. I know it looks silly to be walking over the Little Sugar Loaf using a pair of adjustable ski sticks, but, please believe me, the comfort in descent is worth the embarrassment and the silly jibes about 'are you expecting snow?'. If you get the chance, borrow a pair to try out — you'll be surprised how helpful they are. Being collapsible they can easily be stowed away before reaching tarmac. I have suggested a stick (or preferably a pair!) where the ground or the path is very rough.

Anything that you carry, as opposed to wear, can most easily be carried in a small rucksack — a 'daysack' in technical terms.

I have occasionally suggested carrying books on birds and plants, and a pair of binoculars, for special walks, but in fact they are worth taking on nearly *all* the walks.

I always carry a camera. The modern compact with a zoom lens from 35 mm to 70 or 80 mm is light, adaptable and easy to use. It can be hung around your neck, ready for action when the cloud fleetingly clears the hilltop, or the setting sun blazes red, or the geese suddenly take off. It will also record the autumn colours of the leaves, the spring blossoms, the purple heather and yellow gorse — and of course your companions!

Rereading this section I hope that the long list of items to wear or carry won't put you off. It is impossible to cater for all occasions and while I don't want you to perspire in Knocksink Wood in fleece, anorak and balaclava, I certainly don't want you to freeze on Croaghanmoira in tee-shirt and shorts. In the end, it is up to you to use a little common sense. Don't rush out and buy a lot of gear. Start with the walks that need only what you already possess, and work up. There are good shops for walking gear in Dublin and other towns, where you can get good gear — and good advice. Do remember when choosing that you can always take off a layer if you are too hot, but there is no easy remedy if you are too cold. Always carry something to drink, some emergency food and a small First Aid pack.

Finally I had better say that in the very unlikely event of your needing rescue, there are two highly efficient Mountain Rescue teams in the Dublin–Wicklow area — call 999 or 112.

The forty plus thirty-five walks described are not the only short walks around Dublin. The parks around Dublin offer good short walks — and they are all in reach of public transport. There are other possibilities, and on page xix I've included a very short section with suggestions, and also some suggestions in the Bibliography.

I've enjoyed walking for more than seven decades, and I hope to go on doing so for another few years (a decade is too much to hope). I've enjoyed the research for this book, and I hope you will enjoy using it. Good walking!

Joss Lynam
29 June 2003

Respect the countryside

- Protect wildlife, plants and trees — do not pick flowers
- Take your litter home with you
- Do not pollute water supplies
- Respect farmland
- Don't interfere with farm animals
- Leave all gates as you find them
- Don't block entrances when parking

The Walks by Duration

One Hour or Less

Two Hours or Less, but More than One Hour

Over Two Hours

The Walks by Characteristics

Note: Most walks will come into two or even three categories. The Murrough and Broad Lough for example combine coast and nature, while many of the hills are approached through woods which have their own interest. Walks falling into more than one category are marked with an (*).

Flat!

By their nature all coast walks (see next heading) are flat:

Donadea Forest Park, p. 15
Ballinafagh Lake (*), p. 18
Robertstown — Four Canals (*), p. 21

Dodder Linear Park (*), p. 25
Knocksink Wood (*), p. 42
Glendalough Lakes (*), p. 90

Coast

Laytown and Bettystown Beach (*), p. 1
Coast Walk to Portrane (*), p. 4
Malahide Estuary and Newbridge Demesne (*), p. 8

North Bull Island from Bull Wall (*), p. 11
Kilcoole Nature Reserve (*), p. 52
The Murrough and Broad Lough (*), p. 55

Canals, Lakes and Rivers

Ballinafagh Lake (*), p. 18
Robertstown — Four Canals (*), p. 21
Dodder Linear Park (*), p. 25

Glendalough Lakes (*), p. 90
Art's Lough (*), p. 116

Woodland

Note: Most of the hill walks rely on Coillte woods to get from the public road to the open hillside. I have only included them in this section if the woodland has its own interest or is predominant.

Donadea Forest Park, p. 15
Saggart Hill (*), p. 33
Knocksink Wood (*), p. 42
Silsean (*), p. 73
Church Mountain (*), p. 77

Carrick Mountain (*), p. 81
Glendalough — The Spink (*), p. 87
Between Glendalough and Laragh (*), p. 93
Avondale Forest Park (*), p. 103

Woodland continued

Small Hills and Easy Height Gains

Bigger Hills and Bigger Height Gains

Historical, Social Interest

Nature Interest

Some Other Walks

The thirty-five walks described in this book are not the only walks within easy reach of Dublin. For starters, there are the forty walks described in my *Easy Walks near Dublin* and there are others.

The public parks all offer pleasant strolls:

Ardgillan Castle, Newbridge Demesne, Malahide Castle, Ward River Linear Park, Tolka Valley Park (Fingal County);

St Anne's Park, Phoenix Park, Bushy Park (Dublin City Council);

Marlay Park, Mount Merrion Park, Killiney Hill Park, Cabinteely Park (Dun Laoghaire Rathdown County);

Tymon Park, Corkagh Demesne (South Dublin County).

The canals offer good walks — the Royal in particular because the railway runs alongside and provides good public transport. Don't start too close to Dublin though!

The South Wall of the Liffey and the Dun Laoghaire piers are both recommended for clearing hangovers.

There are plans to develop the Boyne Towpath from Slane.

There should be a good walk in the Glen of the Downs area when the road is complete.

Croaghan Kinsella, furthest outpost of the Wicklow Mountains, fulfils all my criteria — except distance from Dublin — but it is still accessible in a day.

The Walks Accessible by
Public Transport

The following walks can be done reasonably easily by public transport. I haven't included those which are served by one passing bus a day. The details of using public transport are included in the walk description but you do need to check bus times carefully, remembering that weekend services are often less frequent than weekday ones. An (*) means that services are not very frequent, so you need to plan carefully, or be prepared to hang around. For instance the invaluable St Kevin's bus only does one trip each way per day.

Iarnród Éireann (Irish Rail) (main line and DART services)
Connolly Station, Dublin 1. Tel: 353 (0)1 836 6222. Website: www.irishrail.ie

Bus Átha Cliath (Dublin Bus) (Dublin area)
59 Upper O'Connell Street, Dublin 1. Tel: 353 (0)1 873 4222. Website: www.dublinbus.ie

Bus Éireann (Country buses)
Central Bus Station, Store Street, Dublin 1. Tel: 353 (0)1 836 6111. Website: www.buseireann.ie

St Kevin's Bus Service (Dublin–Glendalough)
Roundwood, Co. Wicklow. Tel: 353 (0)1 282 8119

No Extra Walking Time

Laytown and Bettystown Beach (*), p. 1
Coast Walk to Portrane (*), p. 4
Malahide Estuary and Newbridge Demesne, p. 8
Dodder Linear Park, p. 25
Glendalough Lakes (*), p. 90
Between Glendalough and Laragh (*), p. 93
Paddock Hill (*), p. 97

Less than One Hour Extra Walking Time

One Hour, Less than Two Hours

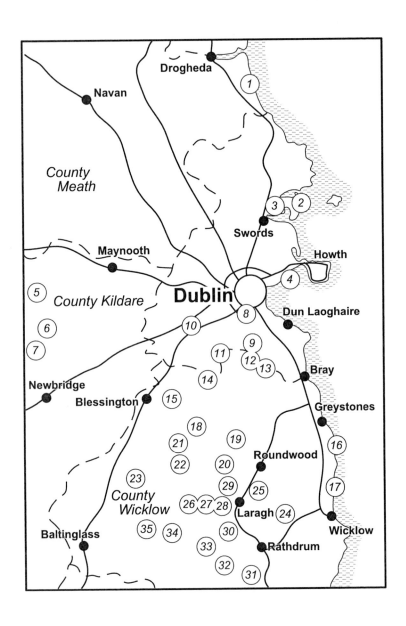

1. Laytown and Bettystown Beach

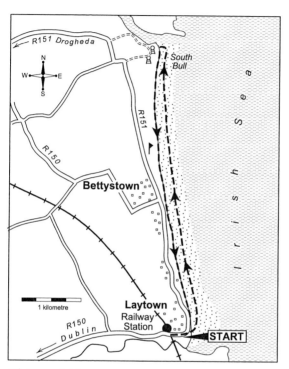

Distance: 10 km
Ascent: Negligible
Time: 2½ hours
Equipment: OSI Discovery Sheet 43. Trainers or walking shoes, rain gear.

This is a pleasant, undemanding walk on one of the country's most famous beaches, from the village of Laytown to the mouth of the Boyne at Mornington. The two strands of Laytown and Bettystown are, in reality, one. Laytown strand is the site of an annual race meeting each summer, the only official such meeting in Britain or Ireland held on a beach.

1

While it is a fairly simple matter to drive from Dublin, it makes a lot more sense to take the train. There is a regular service from Connolly Station; journey time is 45 minutes each way.

Alight at Laytown, the last coastal station on the line before it bends inland towards Drogheda. You are travelling on a part of the original Great Northern Line, which first joined Dublin and Belfast in 1855. It still serves that purpose, as well as providing commuter services to Dublin for dormitory towns as far away as Dundalk.

As you leave the station, you turn left to pass under the bridge that carries the railway. This brings you into the little village and leads directly to the beach. If you are arriving at around lunch time and had reckoned on getting something to eat here before beginning, be warned. During weekdays at least, none of the pubs in Laytown offer lunch although the situation may improve on summer weekends.

At any rate, there is no need to panic. The hotel at Bettystown, barely a half-hour's walk along the beach, will oblige.

It is best to check the tides when planning this walk. Walking on beaches is generally more pleasant at low tide: you have more space at your disposal and, crucially, more hard sand to walk on. Walking on soft, yielding sand can be quite demanding and frustrating. So try to time your walk for an ebb tide.

The route takes you north along Laytown strand. The simplest option is to follow the beach all the way to the end, returning by the dunes that flank the Laytown and Bettystown Golf Club.

Walking in the second half of May, we saw flocks of whimbrels on the beach gathering for their passage north to their breeding grounds in Iceland. This is the best time of year to spot these birds in numbers, although a few will be found right through the summer. Offshore, there were noisy colonies of sandwich terns coming south to breed here. By autumn, they will be gone to their African wintering habitat. There were also a few straggling brent-geese with their distinctive black and white plumage. They are more common in winter; most have departed for the Arctic by early summer.

As you leave Laytown, you can see clear up the coast to the next prominent headland, Clogher Head, which is about 15 km away. On a clear day, the impressive backdrop of the Mourne Mountains will appear clearly on the horizon. The landward side reveals the back gardens of houses that dot the route along as far as Bettystown — some obviously holiday houses, others permanent residences.

Bettystown itself, readily accessible from the beach, has the slightly raffish and provisional air of many seaside places, especially in the low season. From here, the walk continues across level sands northward to the mouth of the Boyne.

The valley of the River Boyne has perhaps the longest continuous record of civilised habitation in Ireland. Barely 15 km inland from the river mouth, the great Neolithic burial sites of Newgrange, Knowth and Dowth mark the site of a pastoral civilisation that flourished as long ago as 3500 BC, making it contemporaneous with the earliest Egyptian pyramids. Yet as we stand here at Mornington, it is not hard to see why this rich river valley failed to become the focus of settlement on the east coast of Ireland and why Dublin Bay and the Liffey, farther to the south, did. There is something apologetic about the manner in which the Boyne meets the sea. There is no broad bay, as at the mouth of the Liffey, to afford a ready anchorage and the focus for a marine settlement. Although the river is navigable and nearby Drogheda is a busy port, it has never challenged Dublin's pre-eminent position.

Most of the return journey to Laytown can be made along the dunes for variety. The views to the south reach as far as the Rockabill lighthouse off the coast at Skerries. The dunes provide nesting sites for skylarks, with their thrilling and never-ending song delivered from on high, an inspiration for poets and dreamers alike. The reality is more mundane: these tiny but resonant song birds are simply marking out their territory, so there is an aggressive intent in the skylark's song that subverts romance. No matter: the sound of the lark in the clear air remains one of the wonders of nature. Hang reality!

The dunes themselves are principally composed of marram grass, and while some small wild flowers will blossom in high summer, there is more to be seen in the area where the dunes and the strand touch. Sea beet, sea spurge, sea spurrey, sea holly and maritime poppies can all be spotted at different times of the year.

There is refreshment to be had in Bettystown, at the three-quarter point of the return journey, and at Laytown itself. From Laytown, you entrain for Dublin and home.

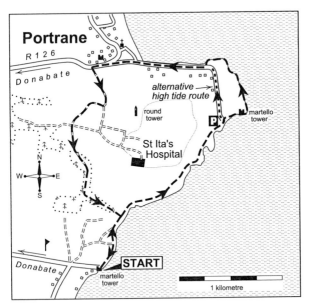

Distance: 5½ km
Ascent: Negligible
Time: 1½ hours
Equipment: OSI Discovery Sheets 43 and 50 (but Sheet 50 will get you to the start and then you can follow the walk quite adequately with the sketch map). Walking shoes, trainers, rain gear, binoculars, bird book.

There are plenty of coastal walks north of Dublin, but nearly all of them are one-way, and you have to return by your outward route, take two cars (or a car and a bike) or fiddle with bus/train timetables. This walk, on the other hand, combines a coast walk with a loop back, partly through a pleasant wood. Don't be put off by the bit of the return that passes close to St Ita's Psychiatric Hospital: we were assured both by a friendly girl in a Portrane village shop and by hospital staff that it's free to walkers — in fact Fingal County Council are considering waymarking it.

Coast Walk to Portrane

Most of the coastal walk is on a sandy path, close to the low cliffs which edge the beach. Halfway along you'll find a sign warning you that the path is dangerous but if you've two legs and at least one eye you shouldn't have a problem! At the Portrane Martello Tower the route does descend to the beach but this section is not passable at high tide and if you don't check the tide table in advance you might have to use the road alternative.

There is quite a variety of bird life (hence the binoculars and bird book) and when I checked the route with a Northsider friend in March (not the best time for birds here — winter is best) we saw cormorants, oyster catchers, scaups and (I think!) bar-tailed godwits.

Take the N1/M1 out of Dublin and, beyond Swords, turn right for Donabate on the R126. In Donabate, pass Smith's pub, and where the main road bears left past the big Catholic church, keep straight on to the coast and a martello tower where there is plenty of parking. You can get to Donabate by bus or rail but it would add 2 km road walk each way, a good hour. Alternatively you could get a 33B bus (not very frequent) to Portrane and start the walk from there, returning by the coast. (See Walk 3 for more information about trains and buses.)

The coast path is obvious beside the hotel and takes you easily and safely along a sandy path near the top of the low cliff, passing a cottage which is obviously someone's dream abode. Low the cliffs may be, but they don't lack interest; dark beds of muddy limestone dipping to the north-east are intermixed with contorted beds of volcanic rock of the Ordovician period, and there are caves too. Out to sea is Lambay, island of mystery to most people since the owners, the Baring family, unfortunately strongly discourage visitors. The architect, Sir Edwin Lutyens, built a house there for the Barings in the early years of the last century, which blends with the Elizabethan house already there and yet has no element of pastiche. He designed all the buildings on the estate to create an architectural masterpiece and I count myself extremely lucky to have been able to visit the island in the course of my work as an engineer. The island is an important archaeological site and also boasts, believe it or not, a small herd of wallabies.

On the landward side the view is dominated by the huge red-brick complex of St Ita's Hospital. Then there's a round tower, which I was surprised to see isn't marked in red as an historical monument until I read afterwards that it was built in the nineteenth century by Sophia Evans of Portrane House as a monument to her husband. It would be as attractive as the real thing if it wasn't for a large, squat concrete tower (water tower?) nearby. As you walk, the two seem to change places, and at one moment the slender round tower seems to be sticking out of the top of the squat water tower!

For some time the path lies beside the wall which was once the boundary of Portrane House and now bounds St Ita's. But keep right at every fork, close to the shore, until you reach a large car park, some old coastguard cottages and a martello tower, now a residence with a walled garden. Here you have a choice; take the road which cuts off the corner or descend by steps to the beach, cross a disused lifeboat slip and continue round the point on the beach. It is quite easy walking, but it is not passable at high tide, so I suggest you choose your time, because you will have enough obligatory tarmac on the final stretch into Portrane without adding more unnecessarily. Follow the beach on sand or low rocks round the point and on below a caravan park. Along this stretch we noticed two large boulders of pink conglomerate, presumably brought from afar and dumped by the huge glacial flow which filled the Irish Sea in the Ice Age. The remains of an old boundary wall crosses the beach right down nearly to low-tide mark, and when you have passed it, a whole new vista opens up — the flat coast of Portrane Burrow, the entrance to Rogerstown Estuary and the coast sweeping round to Rush.

Shortly, it becomes preferable to climb up to the main road into Portrane (*Port Reachaun*, the port for *Rechru*, the old name for Lambay), which brings you along above the sandy beach to the entrance to the village. On the right as you enter is a railed-off circle with a large rusty anchor in the middle. This, a notice informs you, is the bower anchor of the *John Tayleur*, recovered recently by divers. She was an emigrant ship out of Liverpool bound for Melbourne in 1854, but wrecked in a storm on the rocks of Lambay with the loss of some 300 lives, including very many women and children. A little way off the actual route, but worth the extra few minutes to take a look, are the ruins of the 13th-century St Catherine's Church and nearby Portrane Castle, a fortified tower house, probably also 13th-century. They were both part of the estate of the religious community of Grace Dieu, broken up at the Suppression of the Monasteries.

Continue through the small village on the Donabate road and turn left through the imposing railed gate of St Ita's. Go past some houses and a field and take the first turn right along a narrow road which swings round to the left and carries on straight through a crossroads. The main buildings of St Ita's are on the left and you pass the Nurses' Home on the right. The road enters woodland and the noise of water on your right turns out to be a modern sewage farm hidden in the trees. The road becomes a narrow, cobbled path through a delightful strip of woodland, bears round to the left and emerges onto open ground in sight of your outward route, not far from the 'dream abode'. Follow your outward route back in ten minutes or so to the martello tower, your car and refreshment in the hotel.

3. Malahide Estuary and Newbridge Demesne

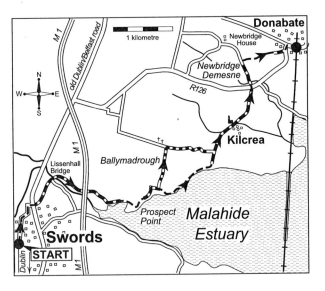

Distance: 7 km
Ascent: Negligible
Time: 2 hours (including a little bird-watching)
Equipment: OSI 1:50,000 Sheet 50. Trainers or walking shoes, rain gear, binoculars, bird book. (My companion on this walk wore toeless sandals without any problems.)

Malahide Estuary is one of the best birding sites near Dublin and it is particularly worth visiting in winter. Although a substantial length of the south shore can be followed in a grassy park, there is a buzz of motor traffic quite close, so I have preferred the north shore which has the added bonus of including the Newbridge demesne (and House if you like) and the finish in the attractive small town of Donabate. You should check the opening hours of the park with Fingal County Council and the more limited hours of the House and restaurant. Another plus for this walk is that in some ways it is easier by public transport than by car — unless of course you have two cars or a car and a push bike!

Take one of the several buses which go to Swords and walk along North Street to the northmost roundabout ('Estuary Roundabout') on the bypass. The 33A or 33B which go through Swords actually have a stop about 200 m before the roundabout. Cross the bypass by the footbridge and walk down Spittal Hill, between the GAA ground and the sewage farm. The road here is flat and the name refers to a leper hospital which in the Middle Ages stood on the hill at the west end of the road. (The first abbot of the monastery at Swords, St Columba, was reputedly a leper.) Keep straight on across the bridge (Lissenhall Bridge) over the Broad Meadow River. In spite of encroaching suburbanism and the motorway, the view downstream leaning on the bridge parapet is still of banks lined with trees, their branches arching over a gently flowing river.

The road bears right (the branch to the left just leads to factories) and passes under the viaduct which carries the new M1 over Broad Meadow. Anyone with an interest in civil engineering will appreciate the method by which the precast spans are launched and temporarily supported; others, like my companion, may wrinkle up their noses at the disfigurement of a beautiful marsh area. Fortunately, the renowned estuary swans don't seem put out and we found them happily at their ease about 200 m below the bridge among the channels which wander through the marshland to the estuary itself. (See the end for birds you are likely to see in the various seasons — the swans are there all year round.) The road gradually deteriorates and finally disappears below the water (the OSI map is optimistic here), but a path climbs onto a wall which leads round Prospect Point where wide views down the estuary to the railway bridge open up. The path is a bit overgrown at one point and you would want to hold on to small children, but this is only for 20–30 m. The wall descends gently to join the re-emerging road which crosses a small stream. Notice the tidal flap over the mouth of the river which prevents the low-lying meadows behind the bank from being flooded in times of high water. The tarmac passes Newport House and turns inland as Ballymadrough Road. However, except at high tide, you should continue along the pebbly beach beneath a stone retaining wall. You can have a small frisson of excitement as the band of seaweed which marks the top-tide level approaches the foot of the wall but there is no danger at all of being cut off, and if you are stopped by the tide you can easily return to Ballymadrough Road and take the first turn right off it to rejoin the main route of the walk.

The beach has pleasant views across the estuary towards Malahide and after it has passed round two bluffs it widens and tarmac appears once again. Turn inland along the tarmac road. Very soon a road comes in on the left — the high tide variant! Continue along the quiet tree-lined road through the small village of Kilcrea until you reach the main road from Swords to Donabate. Directly opposite are the fine gates of an entrance to Newbridge Park. Cross this road — be careful, heavy traffic — to the pedestrian gate. If the park is closed you will have to walk the road into Donabate, so check the closing times carefully! Enter the demesne and after a few minutes walk along a path through wood and grassland you come to a junction right-signposted to Donabate. If you want to see more of the demesne keep straight on and the path will bring you to the House and restaurant, otherwise follow the Donabate sign which brings you out to a small green in front of the Anglican church. A couple more minutes walking brings you over a bridge to the railway station, a welcome pub and the centre of Donabate. The name comes from *Domhnach bát*, the church of the boat or ferry. There's a fine large red-brick Catholic church, but it's a lot younger than the name! To return, either take the 33B bus back through Swords, or (if you have timed your arrival right) take the train which connects to the DART at Malahide.

Some birds to watch out for:
(this is not a complete list)
All year:
   Grey heron, mute swan, shelduck, mallard, oystercatcher, curlew, gulls
Autumn:
   Passage waders and terns, ruff, curlew sandpiper
Winter:
   Brent-goose, shelduck, pochard and other ducks, dunlin, godwits and other waders
Spring:
   Late wildfowl, waders, terns

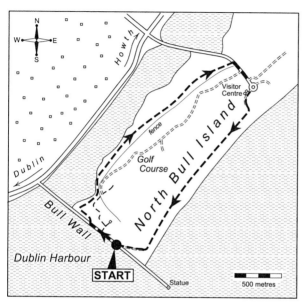

Distance: 6 km
Ascent: Negligible
Time: 1¾ hours
Equipment: OSI Discovery Sheet 50 or OSI Dublin Street Guide. Boots (or possibly wellies), rain gear, bird and flower books, binoculars.

In my last book I described a walk round the northern end of the Island, but the southern end is equally interesting. The North Bull Island is a fairly new addition to Ireland; it only grew from a small sandbank in the last two hundred years, following the construction of the South Wall and then the Bull Wall which created the tidal currents that caused the deposition of sand. The construction of the causeway in 1976 is causing further changes. If you enjoy this walk say a thank-you to Captain William Bligh who designed the Walls to stop silting in the Liffey and in the process gave Dublin a UNESCO Biosphere Reserve (as well as two

11

golf courses, which many of us would rate less highly than the Reserve).
Perhaps all this somewhat balances his behaviour on the Bounty. *It is*
very much a nature walk, and for the birds you must walk in winter, as
we did when I checked the walk. A strong, cold south-west wind, a clear
blue sky, white horses in the Bay and great views made it a wonderful
walk, though I must admit that if it had been less windy we might have
stopped to watch more birds than we did. In summer you will find a
varied and interesting flora, but there is less birdlife. But even if you have
no interest in birds, this is a great invigorating walk, the first half along
a rather rough track just outside the eastern fence of the Golf Club, the
return brisk along the firm sandy beach. For the best view of the birds go
at half tide or a little above — at low tide they are too far away from the
track. (Any serious student of bird or plant life should look out for the
study of the natural history of the North Bull published by the Royal
Dublin Society in 1977, ISBN 0–86027–001–7 or 002–5.) There's also
Flowers of the North Bull *by Dorothy Forde, published by Dublin City*
Council, available at the Interpretive Centre.

By car take the coastal Howth Road out of Dublin and, just where
Clontarf turns into Dollymount, turn right at the traffic lights onto
the wooden bridge that leads to the North Bull. The road drops
down off the Bull at a group of buildings and there is plenty of space
for parking. If you come by public transport, the 130 or (rare) 32X
bus stops near the shore end of the bridge. No need to walk as far
as the car park, just leave the road at the first buildings (one is a
scouts' den) to join the route from the car park — this will only add
minutes to the walk.

At the car park it's worth looking at Dublin Port and Dock's
Information Board about the two Walls before you set off. Walk
back towards the mainland on a broad grassy track below the Bull,
crossing the road leading to the imposing Royal Dublin Golf Club
House and continuing to the scouts' den. For the first part of your
northerly walk you are on top of a low wall but this ends soon where
the fence of the Golf Club projects, and the rest of this part of the
walk is on a rough semi-track with puddles next to the fence. We
walked in strong shoes after heavy rain without getting wet feet, but
boots would be preferable.

However, this is where the bird life begins to be interesting.

Away across the marshes you can see flocks of oystercatchers (at peak over 2,000), dunlins (6,000), redshank and many other waders, while amongst the many cries of the birds you will often distinguish the melancholy note of the curlew. There are plenty of ducks amongst which shelduck, wigeon and teal are the commonest. Gulls (herring, black headed and greater black backed) are omnipresent, as are hooded crows. We were fortunate to see a flock of brent-geese grazing just inside the Golf Course fence — natural mowing machines?

Continue along the vague track on the edge of the marsh, keeping an eye out — we spotted two grey herons and then two little egrets (now extending their range northwards as the globe warms). You may venture into the salt marsh, but don't go too far in, it disturbs the birds. In summer you will find, working inward from the sea, glasswort (*Salicornia sp.*) with its striking autumn colour, the grass *Puccinellia maritima* and thrift (*Armeria maritima*), a mass of pale pink flowers in June. The track improves as you approach the causeway where you join the footpath beside it, which leads quickly to a roundabout. In the middle is a big hoarding with pictures of the commonest birds and flowers, which may be a bit of a let-down after the rarities you think you have seen.

Walk down the road past the Interpretive Centre (well worth a visit, though often closed) and continue to the beach. On a summer day you have to dodge the cars, whose drivers can't resist the thrill of driving on the hard, smooth sand, but after a couple of hundred metres their passage is blocked by a barrier of boulders. Now you can stop to admire in peace the view of the cusps of Dublin, Howth Head to the east and Dalkey to the south. Between, you will almost certainly see freighters heading in and out of Dublin Port, and perhaps a speeding HSS. In winter you may regret the cold wind, but it offers the spectacle of waves breaking far out and swirling up the beach in a tide of foam. Carefully keeping onshore of the tide there will often be flocks of gulls, oystercatchers, dunlins and sanderlings, these last scurrying so fast you can't see their legs move. It is now an invigorating walk along the smooth beach to the distant Bull Wall, noting that the Council has erected picnic tables at intervals, which look like they must be swept away by the tide. The dunes on your right are colonised first by sand sedge (*Carex arenaria*) and then by marram grass (*Ammophila arenaria*), but if you explore inland in summer you will find a variety of flowering plants, including several species of orchid.

When you reach the Bull Wall, if you are still feeling energetic, walk out along the top of the Wall (passing bathing shelters delicately labelled for 'Ladies' and 'Men') to the statue of the Virgin Mary erected in 1972 on a tall tripod. This diversion, there and back, won't take you more than about 10 minutes. To finish the walk turn right and follow the sandy road below the Wall back to the car park. If you came by bus continue along the sandy track below the Wall to meet your outgoing route at the scouts' den.

Car-based walkers may like to turn towards Howth and go onto the Causeway, where it is possible to bird-watch very successfully from your car.

For all, Clontarf offers a variety of refreshment.

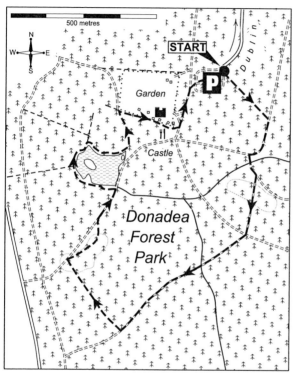

Distance: 3½ km
Ascent: Negligible
Time: ¾ to 1 hour
Equipment: Any good road map for access. Walking shoes or trainers, rain gear.

Donadea is a delightful forest park about an hour's drive from Dublin. 'What!' you say, 'I'm expected to drive for an hour each way just for a short walk.' The answer is 'Yes, and I don't think you'll regret it!' It is the demesne of Donadea Castle, once the home of the Aylmer family (see also Walk 7) and now a Coillte Forest Park. The old castle, Protestant church and garden are closed, but the park itself is very attractive. It is mixed woodland, with many old broadleaved trees and fine mature conifers, and a lake as a centrepiece. Coillte has done much to make it attractive to visitors with good paths, bridges and benches. I have described one particular route which picks out some of the best bits of the park, but you can explore further (the sketch map shows other possibilities), there is a Nature Trail leaflet (available in the coffee shop), and finally there is a wheelchair trail. Quite a lot of the walk is on forest roads, but wherever possible I have taken you onto narrower woodland paths. If you are going there on a Sunday, I suggest you go fairly early, it gets crowded on a fine afternoon, with small children on pink bicycles and blue pedal cars swooshing all round the lake. If you know an orienteer get him/her to loan you the O-map of the Park which is A4 in size and so can fit in more detail than I can find room for on a page of this book.

Get out of Dublin along the N4/M4, and leave it at the exit marked Maynooth/Naas. At the roundabout turn south along the road (R406). Turn right at the first crossroads (impossible to miss, there is a huge electrical distribution centre just beyond with a dozen or more pylons). Follow this road through two main crossroads and a T-junction and you will come to the Forest entrance. Drive in and park at the large car park near the garden wall of the Castle.

Start the walk at the middle of east (left-hand side) of the car park where a broad path heads south-east. Actually the only tricky bit of navigation is starting on this path, it is little vague to begin with! Anyway the path will bring you through mixed woodland to a forest road, where you turn right. This road bears right to a junction, where you turn left, cross a bridge over a dyke and turn right almost immediately at another junction. After all that hectic activity your forest road takes you straight through a crossroads and on past some new conifers into an area of mature broadleaved trees, first on your left, and then on both sides.

Very soon after you are in this mature wood a path goes off to the right and winds pleasantly amongst the trees, eventually meeting a forest road. Turn right along this road which will take you to the lake. If you want to keep off the road I can recommend you walk through the open wood along a ridge paralleling the road on the right side and then drop down from the end of the ridge back to the road and the lake. Turn left along the lake shore — this is where you are likely to meet the crowds. The lake is shallow and reedy, and there are plenty of mallard and perhaps a coot to see. The track goes round two sides of the lake, crosses a footbridge, and goes along the third side with the lake on one side and grassy sward on the other to the corner where there is a pile of stones especially suitable for small children to climb and fall off. Turn left and woodland paths will take you the garden wall where, turning right, a track will bring you to the corner and the castle. A road on your left will take you back to your car, but it's far better to turn right across the old Castle lawn to the coffee shop which serves excellent soup, scones, tea and coffee. This will give you the strength to walk the last couple of hundred metres to your car.

If you want more exercise, I suggest you get the Nature Trail leaflet in the coffee shop and follow all or part of the Trail. The leaflet will tell you a lot more about the trees than I can.

If you do have an invalid (or a pink bicycle) in your party there is a pleasant, short, waymarked trail suitable for wheelchairs from the car park past the coffee shop, round the lake and back

If you need stronger drink, the nearest pub is in Clane. When you leave Clane, make sure you get back toward Maynooth on your outward route; there is another road but it doesn't connect to the motorway.

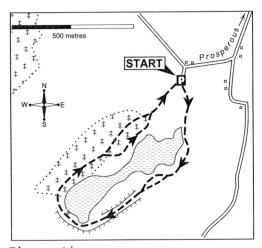

Distance: 3 km
Ascent: Negligible
Time: 1 hour plus viewing time
Equipment: OSI Discovery Sheet 49. Boots or perhaps wellies, rain gear, sticks quite useful, bird and plant books.

This lake, north of Prosperous, is actually the old reservoir of the Blackwood feeder of the Grand Canal. It was built in the 1780s, and as well as acting as a reserve to the Milltown Feeder from Pollardstown Fen, it was used to bring down turf from the bog. It was closed in 1952 as it was no longer needed. Recently it has become a Nature Reserve and simple access paths have been cut. I had never known about it as a possible walk until a friend mentioned it, and on the 1:50,000 map it doesn't stand out. There is a main path right round, with subsidiary paths taking you to the lake itself. I think they were all created simply by cutting the vegetation and leaving it to the trample of feet to make the path. As a result there is a certain amount of tussock hopping and some awkward steps, especially on the return (west side). So you might like a stick or sticks. In winter there are many birds; in spring and summer there are plenty of flowers,

mostly common, though I'm assured there are orchids (see lists at end).
There are enormous beds of brambles, so the blackberry season might be
a good time to visit and there are some raspberries too. We had fun seeing
how many flowering plant species we could identify, and that might be a
good game if there are children in the party — bring the plant and bird
books, but whatever you do, please don't pick the flowers!

The longer but simpler approach is to head out along the N4, turn
off for Celbridge and continue (R403) through Clane to Prosperous.
In the village turn right, after nearly 1 km keep left at a Y-fork and
after a further 2 km, as you descend a small hill, turn left along a
narrow road. Pass a ruined Protestant church with an interesting
tombstone and finally bear right at a junction to reach a car park on
the left, overlooking the lake. It is quicker to take the M5 to the
Maynooth junction and use the R406 and the R408. This is too
complicated to follow by written instructions, but you can find it
with the aid of Sheet 49 and a road map.

Go left out of the car park onto a grassy but rather boggy track
between waist-high brambles, nettles and bracken. This soon leads
to the lake shore which you can follow for a short distance until the
path swings away from the reedy, marshy edge. The next stretch to
the far end is typically a mixture of lush, ground vegetation with
scattered hawthorn, silver birch and willow. Narrow side-paths bring
you closer to the lake, but there is no defined shore, just reed beds
with here and there the tall spear heads of bullrushes. (Around here
you should have your nature books out!) As you approach the south
end the path is on an embankment between the lake and low-lying
meadows and bogland.

The path turns west along the earth dam retaining the lake and
you find the old stone-faced outfall with two valves and control
house close by. Growing on the wall of the outfall you can see the
harts tongue fern, and elder trees overlook it. The elevation of the
dam provides a wide view over the lake, its wooded western shore
and the surrounding country.

At the end of the dam the path turns north through woodland.
This is a delightful walk along a winding path amongst birch and
willow with a greater variety of flowers including yellow irises. Again
you can divert to the right towards the lake from the main path

Ballinafagh Lake

along often vague and sometimes boggy pathlets. It is easy to get disorientated amongst the woods and patches of bogland but be reassured, the main path is out there to your left all the time, and a couple of house roofs are visible to show you that civilisation isn't far away. By one path or another you emerge onto open ground and the car park is plainly visible.

You can rehydrate in Prosperous or Clane.

Two *very* amateur botanists saw the following plants in early June: speedwell, herb robert, ragged robin, clovers, buttercup, heather, lesser stitchwort, cat's ear, ox-eye daisy, white bedstraw, meadow pea, tormentil, sorrel, silverweed, common horsetail, and those mentioned in the text.

Birds which may be seen: black-headed gulls (breeding?), mallard, little grebe, snipe, redshank. Marsh harriers have been seen and also whooper swans, judging by the name of a nearby house.

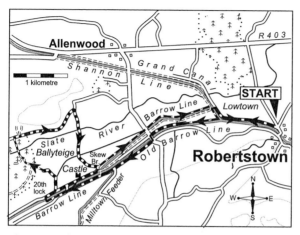

Distance: 8 km
Ascent: Negligible
Time: 2 hours
Equipment: OSI Discovery Sheet 49 and/or Grand Canal Guide. Walking shoes/light boots, rain gear.

The canals that cross Ireland are an important part of our history, and what better place to look at them than around Robertstown where the Grand Canal, Barrow Old and New Lines and the Milltown Feeder meet, each with a different slice of history. Robertstown itself is aware of its history and has developed the fine hotel which provided an overnight stop for passenger boats in the first half of the nineteenth century into a Canal Museum and Centre. When it was built the canal boats offered the quickest means of passenger travel but when the railway provided a faster service, the hotel closed in 1849 and had many uses before being restored. Robertstown is a thriving village with food and drink readily available and plenty of parking. The canals were all busy with freight in the nineteenth century and were still viable in the first half of the twentieth. Certainly Guinness Brewery made good use of them, malt coming in from the Barrow, and stout going out west. The route I

(side tab:) Robertstown — Four Canals

describe takes a look at all four waterways and it can be shortened or lengthened according to taste. There is rather a lot of tarmac because most of the towpaths are surfaced but it is often possible to walk on the grass edging. For two women we met while I was checking out the walk, its great virtue was that it was flat; it is certainly a change from the mountain walks in this book.

Take the N4/M4 out of Dublin and turn off at the first exit (signposted Celbridge) from the motorway section. At the next roundabout take the R405 into Celbridge, then the R403 through Clane to Prosperous. At the far end of Prosperous turn right onto an unnumbered road to Kilmeage/Robertstown. Follow this across the Grand Canal (Bonynge Bridge) and turn right at the next crossroads and so reach Robertstown. Park in the village (or if there's no space, use a car park a little beyond the village on the south side of the canal). Robertstown is also accessible from Naas.

The walk starts at the Binn's Bridge over the Grand Canal in the middle of the village, typical of the many humpback canal bridges. Cross the bridge and at the fourway junction keep left onto the towpath which you follow to Lowtown. You are beside the first of the four canals of the day's walk, the Grand Canal, which is 131 km long with 43 locks, from Ringsend to Shannon Harbour. Built between 1772 and 1805 by a private company, the Grand Canal Company, it was the most successful of the Irish canals and was quite busy up to 1950 when it was nationalised under CIE. It finally closed for commercial traffic in 1960, but has always remained open for recreational traffic, avoiding the fate of the Royal Canal, much of which was dewatered (though it is now being restored). The towpath leads you to Fenton's Bridge and Lowtown, the busy junction of the Grand Canal and the Barrow Line.

As you cross the bridge, the 19th Lock, the lock which starts the long descent to the Shannon, is immediately on your left. (It is a little hard to accept that the section we have just followed is the 'summit level', all of 82 m above sea level.) A yellow man of the Barrow Way tells you turn left beyond the bridge and join the towpath beside the Old Barrow Line, second of the four canals. This canal which connected the Grand to the Barrow Navigation at Athy was completed in 1791, but in fact this 'Old Line' was closed in

1804 to save water. Anyway, the towpath is a pleasant, unsurfaced track which brings you in a kilometre or so to Harberton Bridge, which, following the yellow man, you cross to get onto the surfaced towpath on the other bank. There's a pub here, by the way.

Another kilometre brings you to Huband Bridge, which takes you over the Milltown Feeder, the main source of supply of water to the canals. It counts as our third canal since it is navigable for light draft boats (0.75 m) as far as the intriguingly named Point of Gibraltar. The source of this feeder is the many springs in Pollardstown Fen, a unique example of a landscape and flora that was widespread in Ireland 5,000 years ago. It is now a Nature Reserve. It can make a pleasant walk in itself (see Walk 7 in *Easy Walks near Dublin*). There was originally another feeder, the Blackwood Feeder, coming in from a reservoir to the north at Bonynge Bridge, but it was closed in 1952. For the circuit of this reservoir see Walk 6.

However, today we continue along the Old Line and in a couple of minutes you reach the old 19th Lock and just beyond it, the new Barrow Line coming in from the far bank, and crossed by a very steep, unusual skew bridge. So now we have our fourth canal, the modern route to the Barrow. (I don't really understand how this new line saved water but all the books agree that it was to save water that it was built.) Continue along the towpath, now beside the new Line, and this is a good moment to look at your surroundings. On our left is the Hill of Allen, one side nearly eaten away by a huge quarry. The rest is wooded and on the summit is a tower, a folly built in the nineteenth century by the Aylmer family (see also Walk 5) on the site of a tumulus. Just across the canal is Ballyteige Castle — you pass it on our return. Further away to the north-west is the cooling tower of the Allenwood peat-fired power station, now closed, having devoured all the peat within easy reach. (By the time you read this guide, the cooling tower may have been demolished.)

The surfaced road takes a kink away from the canal but guided by the yellow man you continue along a gravel track, passing a lock-keeper's house and leaving the Barrow Way to climb up to the 20th Lock, where you cross the canal by the lock gate footway. This is where you start to return and I have brought you this far because it illustrates one of the difficulties the canal builders faced. Severe subsidence in Ballyteige Bog made it necessary to rebuild the canal and move the 21st Lock back from the aqueduct over the Old River. Even now, as you can see, the canal is well above the level of the surrounding land.

Turn back along the towpath, noticing a road signposted Ballyteige going off on the left. If you want to get away from the canal for a bit you can follow this road into the pleasant Ballyteige forest and then taking two right turns, rejoin the canal at the Skew Bridge. Otherwise, continue along the towpath passing Ballyteige Castle. It is a typical tower house of the fourteenth to sixteenth centuries, and probably belonged to the Geraldine family. Unfortunately it is not open. Beyond the Skew Bridge the towpath, now unsurfaced, continues to Littletown Bridge, which is quite close to that pub I mentioned on the outward journey. Beyond the bridge the towpath is unsurfaced and inclined to be muddy. When I checked this route I looked enviously at the path on the far bank, but I don't think there is much to choose between them.

The canal bends and soon you begin to meet boats, and yet more boats, afloat and ashore. Just as the Grand Canal comes in sight again a high footbridge crosses our canal. Climb this and descend into Lowtown Boatyard, where you must thread your way amongst the cruisers being repaired or wintered ashore to come out at the 19th Lock again. In summer probably most of these boats would be afloat and far away. From the lock retrace your steps along the towpath to Robertstown and its welcoming shops and pubs.

Dodder Linear Park

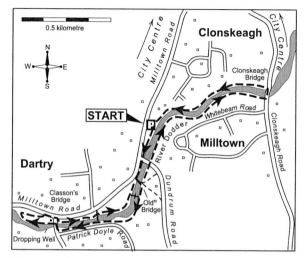

Distance: 3½ km
Ascent: Negligible
Time: 1 hour
Equipment: OSI 1:12,000 Map of Dublin. Trainers, rain gear.

*This is a bit of a cheat, because it is really **in** Dublin, but because it's Nora's and my favourite walk when we haven't much time and don't want to go far, here it is. I'm not including the whole Linear Park, and I'll surely be in trouble with the residents of Rathfarnham for omitting all the interesting stretches up their way, but, sorry, this is our pet area. It is the only long section of the Park that has a path on both sides of the river, so you can make an enjoyable figure-of-eight walk almost without retracing your steps, and as you will find, it has plenty of sights to see.*

Drive to Milltown, either through Ranelagh or Rathmines and park in the car park a little east of Milltown Bridge, at the foot of the hill. The 48A bus will drop you at the same place. This is our traditional start, but using the bus you could as easily start at Classon's Bridge

Dodder Linear Park

(14A) or Clonskeagh Bridge (11). I say 'using the bus' because parking is not so easy at either place unless you have the neck to use a pub car park.

From the Milltown car park walk pleasantly through the grassy park to the bridge, passing amongst fine birches, willows and other trees. Go through the tunnel under the road bridge, and when you come to the old bridge, cross the river. It's a fine stone bridge, and it has an extra arch on the south side for a mill channel. Of an evening you may find some fishermen casting from the bridge. They've told us that they catch trout ... trout? In such polluted water? A fishy story? Turn right along the path, with carefully designated strips for cyclists and pedestrians, to the old mill weir — you can still see the mill channel gate. There's a resident heron here, generally to be seen standing hunched up at one end of the weir waiting for ... trout?

The path continues through grassland beside the river towards the viaduct which now carries the LUAS track. Along here (there *must* be fish!) you can often find a cormorant who has a favourite perching boulder in the river. We have also seen him perched on the top of the old Dargle Laundry chimney, which has now been restored. What is he watching for there — flying fish?

Beyond the newly-cleaned stonework of the viaduct the path rises and becomes the pavement of Patrick Doyle Road, which leads to Classon's Bridge. Cross the road (busy, I'm afraid) and pause to look upstream from the bridge. When I wrote this, in summer 2003, facing upstream in the middle of the river, was a rhinoceros. Very dangerous beasts, we are told, but this one is harmless — he's made of bronze and stands on a concrete pedestal bolted to the bottom of the river. The owner of the Dropping Well denies knowledge of how it got there, but since he also owns another pub which has a bronze horse and a bronze elephant outside, I don't quite believe his denial. Anyway I hope it is still there for you to see it, it's fine sight.

Walk past the Dropping Well, through the car park and continue along the path near the road to the end of the park where the path joins the road. Turn left here, down to the river and another weir, also with the beginning of a mill channel. I've been told there were mills all down the Dodder in this stretch, but I haven't been able to find out anything about them.

Now you turn downstream, beside the river, pass a pair of

bronze cranes outside the back of the pub, go under the bridge and continue along a pleasant path beside the river, overhung with willow trees. The path goes under the viaduct, passes the restored chimney, and continues between the river and some large blocks of new flats, their back gates all sporting warning notices about CCTV. Take another look for the heron at the weir, and then cross the old bridge again.

Turn left off the bridge along the path heading downstream. The imposing modern building on your right is a Muslim Study Centre. The old mill channel (leading, I presume, to the mill that gave Milltown its name) can be seen first on the left of the path and then on the right. There's a stone footbridge blanked off by a wall, and a blanked-off arch where the channel once went under the road — but there's nothing to be seen on the other side of the road. Cross the Dundrum Road (pedestrian lights) and continue along the path beside the river (you are now opposite your starting point). This stretch to Clonskeagh Bridge is perhaps the most pleasant section of the walk. Most of the way there is a fringe of trees beside the river, while on the other side is an old stone wall overhung with trees. This section is in Dun Laoghaire Rathdown County, and (truly!) it was closed during the foot-and-mouth outbreak in 2001, although the rest of the park, in South Dublin County, was open.

The path and the river bear right and close under the wall is what looks like the base of an old street lamp. Both the base and a manhole beside it have the letters 'R N^o1' with 'RDC' below embossed on them, and the lamp base has the date '1911'. There are two more manholes similarly embossed further along. Does 'R' stand for Rathmines, which was a separate authority from Dublin until about 1930, and is this its sewer out to Dublin Bay? A little further on are more intriguing sights. First a blanked-off arch parallel with the river, perhaps the tail-race of the Milltown mill, then another at right-angles to the river. There are also steps which would take you up to Whitebeam Road. The path winds round beside the river, or if you want some soft going for a change, you can take a short cut across the grass, passing the blocked doorways which once gave the residents of Whitebeam private access to the river.

When you reach Clonskeagh Road cross Clonskeagh Bridge and turn left immediately onto a tarmac lane, though not before noting two handy pubs, O'Shea's just beside you, and Ashton's across the road. The lane branches right up to a cottage, and though you can continue along a narrow path just above the river with a low concrete wall to stop you falling in, I recommend you walk past the cottage and follow an unsurfaced path under an arch of trees. The lower path climbs to join you up some steps and you continue, now directly above the river, on a concrete path. On your right, above a steep bank is a wilderness area of trees, bushes and brambles; one wonders how it has escaped a developer. But I've heard planning permission is being sought for houses at the Clonskeagh end and a 'park' at the Milltown end. The path once more dives under an arch of trees and emerges at an open, paved area in front of a row of neat cottages. 'What a lovely place to live!' I've thought of saying to one of the residents, but I'm afraid of the likely retort: 'It would be — if it wasn't for you walkers going past the front door'. Go round the corner from the cottages, and there is the car park.

Refreshments(?) — I've already made enough suggestions!

9. Fairy Castle and Three Rock Mountain

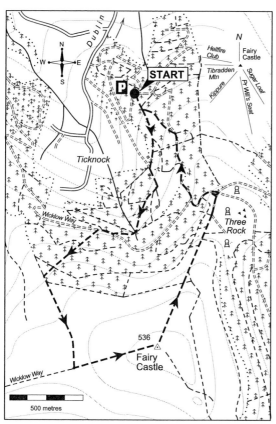

Distance: 5 km
Ascent: 240 m
Time: 2 hours
Equipment: OSI Discovery Sheet 50. Boots, weather gear; sticks preferable if you are at all unsteady on rough ground.

Everybody in Dublin knows Three Rock, or as I, rather sadly, now call it, 'Nine Mast Mountain', though by the time you walk there, it may be

29

'Ten Mast'! It is easy of access and a fine viewpoint over the city, especially in the evening when the lights come on. The route I am suggesting is a circuit which is more interesting than the traditional straight up and back from the car park. It is all on track, but a lot of the tracks are quite rough, being favourite challenges for mountain bikes and even motor bikes. What bike wheels have started the heavy rains of summer 2002 have made worse, and hence my recommendation of boots and maybe also sticks. It can be crowded at the weekend, but it is a nice walk for a summer evening, and going the way I'm suggesting, the return route is on a good gravel track looking down on the city. The OSI map is on too small a scale to show the tracks through the woods accurately; you must use the sketch map, or if you know any orienteers, try to cadge a Three Rock O-map (1:10,000) from them.

From the city take the R117 road through Dundrum (Main Street) to the Sandyford crossroads, turn right onto the R113, go past the Lamb Doyle's pub and just before the road crosses over the M50, turn sharp left, up the road signposted Ticknock. If you are coming from the west city, you can reach the same point by driving up the R113 in the other direction, from Marlay Park. Now keep going straight, towards Ticknock, passing a road on the right, until you come to the forest entrance.

At the forest entrance there is a gate, closed at night. There's a noticeboard to tell you what time the gate is closed (varying at time of writing from 4 pm in winter to 8 pm in high summer). If you think you won't be back in time, park at the entrance; if you have time in hand, drive into the forest, keeping right at the junction just inside and follow the forest road in a wide sweep right and then left to an open, gravelled parking area with a closed gate at the top. Park here. If you have to park at the entrance it will add an extra 15 minutes or so to the walk (on foot you needn't follow the forest road, there are straighter tracks through the wood). You could do this walk using the 44 bus to Sandyford and walking past Lamb Doyle's to the Ticknock junction, but it is a busy road and would add over an hour, and not a pleasant one, to the walk.

The start is up a stony track on the right, just at the corner where the forest road widens into the car park. The track plunges into the wood, and quickly improves. Very soon you take a right fork, and after about 150 m a second right fork. This fork leads you out into the open at a big junction, where you take the track that passes in front of an old corrugated-iron shed. This belongs to the firing range which you can see up on the gorsy hillside on your left. The track climbs up beside the wood and at the next fork you go right again into the wood along a gently rising track which unfortunately has been very much pitted by water and bikes. Follow this track, ignoring any branches, cross a small stream and join a good road running along the border between the mature forest you were in and a steep slope of young trees. Turn right along this road for 100 m or so, to a Wicklow Way yellow man and an arrow pointing up a steep rough track on the left. It looks dire but very soon improves and takes you slanting up through young trees, across two junctions. At the second junction the Wicklow Way inexplicably turns right, but we continue along to open ground where we rejoin the Way. Turn left and follow a good path carved from the slope of deep heather, beside an old boundary wall. The slope eases and you come onto the top of the broad ridge and new views to the south of Prince William's Seat and the other hills beyond Glencullen. The walking man signals right, on his way to Glencullen and beyond, but we turn left. Just at this junction, by the way, there is a nice flat-topped boulder, which, as we found on the day I checked this walk, makes a nice seat for two to eat their lunch. (There isn't another handy stopping place for a long way.)

The main track ahead of you has been badly misused by bikes, but there is a narrower one on its right which, though stony, makes quite good walking. It leads straight along the ridge, rising and then easing off to the big cairn of the Fairy Castle, 536 m, the summit of the walk, and a fine viewpoint. A wood blocks most of the view east, but from the Great Sugar Loaf in the south-east the view swings round over Prince William's Seat (Walk 12) to Cruagh Mountain (Walk 11), Tibradden and round and down to Dublin in the north. Near at hand to the east you can see (and take time to visit if you like) the two granite tors that give this area its name of Two Rock. All along this walk you are at the northern end of the great hump of granite which forms the Wicklow Mountains, and which provides lucky Dubliners with a nearby mountain playground that few other capital cities can match.

Take the rough track heading north-east — back towards the city! It is stony and perhaps you will wish the mountains were of some softer rock than granite and certainly you will wish all bikers, motor or pedal, would find somewhere else to prove their skill. But it is a gentle descent, and it soon brings you to the forest of masts and a gravel road.

A couple of hundred metres brings you to a crossroads where you turn sharply left downhill. Over on your right you'll see the three tors that give the mountain its name; again, go and take a look and a scramble if you like. (The tors used to be the place to which Dublin mountaineers would climb to celebrate the New Year.)

Go down the well-travelled gravel road (now you can see the butts of the firing range below you on the left) until mature forest appears on the left. A little further on a left fork through the wood brings you pleasantly back to the start.

You can rehydrate not far away in Lamb Doyle's!

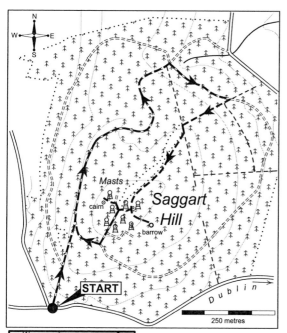

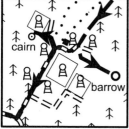

Distance: 3.3 km
Ascent: 90 m
Time: 1¼ hours
Equipment: OSI Discovery Sheet 50. Walking shoes/trainers, rain gear.

There are plenty of small wooded hills near Dublin which are worth visiting, and this is one of them, in spite of the growth of masts on its summit. It offers quite pleasant woodland, some archaeological interest, and at a distance from Dublin which makes it suitable for a winter afternoon or a summer evening. The walking is mainly on good paths but there is a stretch through mature conifer woodland with some brashing to step over. Grandparents may find this stretch a little rough, but the grandchildren will enjoy it! The Irish name Cnoc Theach Sagard *means the hill of the house of Sacra, one of the fathers who composed* The Synod of Armagh *about 696.*

Take the N81 Blessington Road through Tallaght and follow it until you are abreast a lake (Brittas Lake — no name on OSI map) on your right. Then turn right sharply uphill (this is the second turn to the right after the hospital), go straight through a crossroads and climb up towards the hill topped by a radio mast. The road levels out and you can park at a forest entrance where the road takes a sharp left turn. This walk could be done using the 65 bus, asking to be let off at Brittas. At the crossroads take the narrow road heading west, turn left at the T-junction and join the car route. This would add 2 km either way onto the walk, about 1 hour.

Follow the gently-rising forest road through a mixture of old deciduous woodland and mature conifers. Ignore the fork on your left and nod at the turn on your right (that's where you will emerge on your return journey). The road levels out and now runs between young spruce; however, they are well back from the road, you feel you are in the open, and you can catch a view or two through gaps in the planting. The road snakes around through older trees down to a crossroads.

Turn right here along a road through mature wood; it was very pleasant when I last walked here, with the sun dappling the tree trunks. The road veers slightly left to a turning circle with a path on the right which you take. It has been rather messed up by motorcyclists but there is easy walking in the wood beside it. It climbs steadily to meet a fence with a mucky track beyond it. Cross the track and you will see open ground ahead. Even if you can't see it, all you have to do is walk upward through the wood until you reach the open ground. It is fairly easy going, on moss and pine needles although there are some brashings to avoid. The open ground is rough, so, using it as a 'handrail', keep in the wood on its left side until you reach a steel forest in the form of a green hut on your right, a mast in an enclosure on your left, and a surfaced road between.

However, there are some historical attractions to look at. Firstly, go to the south-east corner of the enclosure on your left and start walking away from the enclosure in the direction the railings point. You'll hardly have gone 20 paces before you see ahead of you through the trees a grassy clearing. When you reach it you will find that it is a circular flat-topped mound — the OSI map calls it a ring fort, but to me it looks like a burial barrow. It isn't historically interesting, but I found that to stand in the middle of this perfectly-round, smooth, grassy circle surrounded by trees was a dreamy experience.

Now return to the road and follow its branch to the north-west to another large enclosure; walk along the south-west side to open ground which offers a fine view of the central plain to the north-west, with the low grassy ridges of Windmill Hill, Athgoe Hill and Lyons Hill in the foreground, and some of Dublin's dormitory towns in the background. Just to your left as you walk beside the enclosure is a mound with a central hollow, the remains of a cairn. (The instructions for these little excursions are rather complicated; you should, however, find it easy to follow the small sketch map.)

Now all that remains is to follow the road down through the maze of masts to a T-junction, and turn right (the Wicklow Mountains show up well from here) along a road which quickly brings you to your outward route and so back to the forest entrance. You can rehydrate at the Brittas pub, most easily reached by reversing the public transport route.

11.  Glendoo and Cruagh Mountains

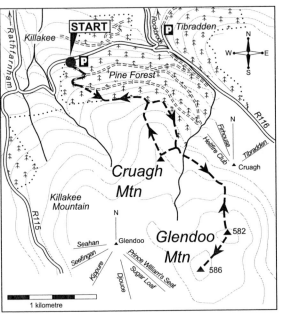

Distance: Glendoo 7 km; Cruagh 4.4 km
Ascent: Glendoo 230 m; Cruagh 170 m
Time: Glendoo 2¼ hours; Cruagh 1½ hours
Equipment: OSI Discovery Sheet 50. Boots, weather gear. For the view south from Glendoo you also need Sheet 56.

These are not the most exciting mountains within reach of Dublin, but they have several advantages which make them worthwhile targets. They are easily accessible from Dublin, there are fences on the open hillside so you can't get lost even if the mist comes down, and there are good views. They were very popular in the early years of the century, and feature in Weston Joyce's The Neighbourhood of Dublin. *He recommends cycling out, but walkers these days will probably prefer a car-borne approach. My companion when I walked these routes related how, in his courting days, he and his wife-to-be would take the 47A bus to*

Rockbrook, walk up to the Pine Forest and then climb Glendoo. Since this would add a good hour-and-a-half to the time taken, I can't recommend it, but it is a possibility! I've grouped the two walks together because they share the one route for more than half the distance and in fact you can combine them. Both are part forest track, part rough path across easy heather slopes. Do stick to the paths — off them you are in deep heather and uneven ground. Cruagh is suitable for an evening walk, but check the closing time of the forest car park (see Introduction).

Take the R116 out of Dublin through Rathfarnham and Rockbrook as it snakes up beside the Owendoher River. About 2 km beyond Rockbrook the road twists sharply as it crosses the river and you come to a T-junction. Bear right and after about 1 km there is a car park in the forest on your left. (Space for cars outside if the car park is likely to be closed when you return.)

Walk up the forest road behind the car park, and turn sharp right, along a gently-rising forest road through pleasant mature conifer woodland with a grassy floor. Turn sharp left at the next bend and follow the road, passing a rough open ride on your right until after 3–4 minutes you reach a track on the right, just beside a turning circle. This track leads you to the edge of the wood, where you turn left onto another rough track. (Make a mental note of this junction because you will be returning by the same route.) This track generally has several puddles in it, hence my insistence on boots. (The puddles can be avoided by some acrobatics on the wooded bank.) This second track veers right and climbs with the forest on the left and heather slopes on the right until it turns to the left at the top of the wood. This is where the routes part.

For **Cruagh** turn right along a fairly narrow path which brings you quickly up to the corner of a newish wire fence. Turn right again onto a narrow path with a decrepit wire fence on your right. Walk a short distance along this and you will see what I am designating the summit of Cruagh Mountain, a post on a mound, 50 m across heather to your left. No path, so pick your way. I say 'I am designating' because the OSI name Cruagh Mountain (*Sliabh na Craobhaí* — the mountain of the large tree) is just sprawled across the hill with no spot height. There is no view to the south but there is a good view north, from the Hellfire Club on the left to Tibradden Mountain and the distant radio masts on Three Rock Mountain on the right. Between, seen over the forest, are massed the southern suburbs of Dublin from Firhouse round to Marlay.

Return to the path and continue along it. After a short while it begins to descend and gets rougher, in fact it isn't sure whether it is a path or a ditch, but this does not last long and soon a big track comes in on the left (shown on the OSI map, coming from Glassamucky Mountain) and a few more metres brings you onto your upward track. Return to the car park by your outward route. For a change you can cut down through the forest to the first junction, but don't try this until you are past the area covered in brashings and can see a faint path through the grassy wood.

Glendoo. Where the Cruagh path turns right, keep straight ahead along a broad rough track beside a fence running away from the forest. (I think this has been cleared of vegetation to act as a firebreak for trees which will be planted on the other side of the fence.) It starts well but gets very muddy and you may prefer a drier path which walkers have created on the right side. At a T-junction of fences the track stops. Continue straight on along a narrow twisty path through the heather beside an old wire fence which will bring you to the summit plateau of Glendoo Mountain, which, to make up for Cruagh, has two spot heights! It also needs two viewpoints, one at each end of the flat summit. From near Pt 582 the view is roughly the same as from Cruagh, but move south to Pt 588 and the North Wicklow hills are all spread out in front of you. To the left is the ridge of peaks from Seahan, Corrig and Seefingan (Walk 14) round to Kippure with its radio masts; in the centre, beyond Glencree, are Tonduff, War Hill, Djouce and Maulin; and far away beyond the Dargle is the pyramid of the Great Sugar Loaf. Finally, cast your eye towards the east, where you lord it by 30 m over nearby Knocknagun and Prince William's Seat (Walk 12).

You return, I'm afraid, by the same route. We explored some alternatives but all turned out to be unpleasant struggles in deep heather, pitted with invisible hollows. To vary it, you can, if you have a little spare energy, return to the bifurcation and walk up Cruagh Mountain. This involves an additional climb of a mere 20 m, and an extra 15–20 minutes.

The discerning will have noticed a pub or two on the road up through Rockbrook.

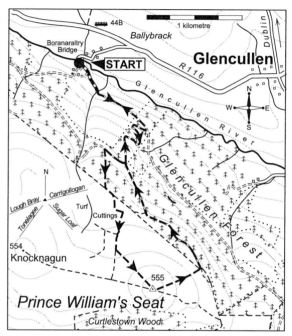

Distance: 7 km
Ascent: 305 m
Time: 2½ hours
Equipment: OSI Discovery Sheets 50 and 56. Boots, weather gear, compass if the cloud is down.

If you have seen my earlier book, Easy Walks round Dublin, *you may remember a walk up Prince William's Seat from Glencree on the south. This route from Glencullen on the north is a tougher proposition. Rather a lot of the walk is on forest roads, but once you get onto the open hillside the tracks are rough and sometimes boggy and the final stretch is bumpy heather. Nevertheless it definitely has its own virtues as an invigorating walk with fine views — perhaps the best panorama in North*

Wicklow. There is another advantage — a bus service up Glencullen means that the walk can quite easily be done using public transport. I can't find the origin of the name — there are many Prince Williams in Anglo-Irish history, but since the name has a distinctly nineteenth-century feel about it, I would make a wild guess and suggest the Prince who later became William IV of England.

Take the Enniskerry Road (R117) through Sandyford and turn off right beyond the new roundabout onto a narrow road signposted Glencullen, along the eastern slopes of Three Rock Mountain which brings you with many twists to a crossroads in Glencullen village beside Fox's pub. (In fact this pub is so well signposted that you can hardly go wrong getting this far.) But at this stage of the day, turn right away from the pub, up Glencullen (R116). This used to be a quiet rural road but it is becoming a rat run between south-east and south-west Dublin, so be careful! After about 1.5 km turn left into the valley. There's no signpost, but there is a yellow man marker to show you that you have joined the Wicklow Way. Park at Boranaraltry Bridge (see Sheet 50) across the Glencullen River (space for 3–4 cars, you need to be an early bird on Sunday!). Do not attempt to drive further, there is a Forestry barrier a short distance up and turning is almost impossible. By bus, take the 44B, ask for Boranaraltry and walk down to the bridge — say an extra half-hour in total. The service isn't frequent — check the times before you set out!

Walk up the road, which soon ceases to be tarmac, through farmland with pleasant views across the valley, past a second barrier to a junction where you turn right up a forest road through young trees (transfer here to Sheet 56). Two zigzags bring you to another junction where you leave the Wicklow Way, turning right along a forest road, with mature trees on your left. About 200 m along this road, turn very sharply left up a rough track which brings you to the edge of the forest.

In front of you are gentle heathery slopes, seamed with the trenchings of abandoned turf cuttings. The tracks which you now follow were made to serve the turf extraction, which means firstly that they don't go where we really want them and secondly they are fairly overgrown. They are also boggy in parts and covered in sphagnum, but most of the messy bits are bypassed by recent narrow paths — look out for these, they aren't always obvious.

Almost immediately after crossing the track which fringes the forest there is a junction; fork left. The track meanders across the boggy hillside as though it hadn't decided where to go and finally climbs resolutely towards some cuttings. Another junction — left again. The third junction is hard to spot. It is about 100 m from the second junction where the track is really getting into the cuttings. Low banks on either side are the most obvious recognition feature of this third track which heads directly for the summit for 100 m or so and turns right. Abandon it and aim for the summit over rough, heathery, tussocky ground, which gradually becomes easier walking as you climb. If you miss that last junction, don't worry; just head for the summit, it just means more rough ground to cross. The summit trig point (555 m) comes in sight, and suddenly, a whole new vista appears — from Three Rock Mountain and its masts to the north, to Kippure in the east with Lower Lough Bray peeping out below it, Mullaghcleevaun, the whaleback of Tonelagee, Djouce, Great Sugar Loaf, Carrigollogan and Killiney Hill — a full 360°. Down in Glencullen you can see the cranes of Ballybrew Quarry, one of the few remaining granite quarries in operation. The fashion for polished granite facing will, we can hope, keep this traditional industry alive (see Walk 21).

Now to pick your path for the descent; it is the leftmost of two going roughly east and easily distinguishable by a line of stones on its left edge (Bearing 72° Magnetic). The path is edged with granite boulders for quite some distance; it certainly isn't a bog road — there are no turf cuttings here. Perhaps it was made to bring the eponymous Prince to his Seat? For whatever purpose it was made, it is easier than the tracks we used in the ascent and brings you quickly to the forest edge and a T-junction.

Go right for a few metres to another T, turn very sharply left onto a good track, and rejoin the Wicklow Way as you re-enter the forest. The forest road contours the slope, descending gradually, with pleasing views of the meadows and woods of Glencullen, now marred somewhat by new housing. A kilometre along this road brings you to the junction with your upward route, which you follow back to your car.

For refreshment or a meal, where else but Fox's pub?

Knocksink Wood

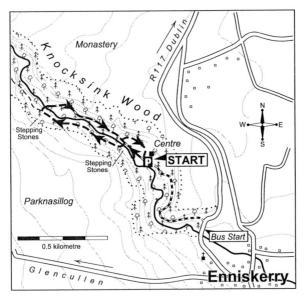

Distance: 2 km
Ascent: Negligible
Time: ½ hour plus dawdling time
Equipment: OSI Discovery Sheet 56. Walking shoes or trainers or gumboots for small kids, rain gear. (But see below if you are crossing the river.)

Knocksink Wood is a Conservation Area just on the Dublin side of Enniskerry and included in it is the National Centre for Environmental Education, which unfortunately is open only for school groups, not the general public. The Conservation Area comprises a long, deep, steep-sided, wooded valley down which flows the Glencullen River. It offers several very pleasant short walks along good paths, with the possibility also of exciting river crossings. It is on the junction of Wicklow granite and limestone, and while this does not obviously affect the scenery it does make for varied flora and fauna, and hence the Conservation designation. It is a curious mixture of care and neglect. There are some carefully tended paths with steps and little bridges made from lengths of small logs yet one of the two sets of stepping stones marked on the map at the Centre is only passable when the river is really low and even then with some difficulty. We checked it out in late March, a good time for the woodland flowers which are hurrying to flower and seed while the trees are still bare and the sunlight can penetrate. Lesser celandine, wood anemone were out in numbers, while primroses and violets were just beginning to bloom. The trees are mostly alder and willow in the rather damp valley bottom, while on the drier slopes the commonest trees are sessile oak with holly and hazel underbrush. A notice board just past the Centre will tell you more about the rarities and the protected species which include red squirrels.

As you will gather from what I write below, it is very much up to you where and how far you walk. It is a popular place, so avoid Sunday afternoon. Even on Sunday morning it can be a bit crowded. The Wood is open from 8.30 am to 5.30 pm from 1 October to 31 March and from 8.30 am to 8.30 pm for the rest of the year.

Take the Enniskerry Road (R117) out of Dublin and where the road forks at the petrol station beyond the Scalp, keep right. The road descends quite steeply and with several bends into the village, and just as it begins to flatten out you will see a sharp turn uphill on your right. Drive in through the gates along a narrow road cut out of the hillside to an open space at the end of the road beside the Centre. Park there. This walk is also easily accessible by the 44 bus, which has a stop a little further along the road towards the centre of the village, near the church. The additional walking time will be about a half-hour altogether.

Go past the barrier and take a look at the notice board — you'll be very clever if you spot a live devil's coach-horse! The road has a hard surface, broad enough for vehicles, but the only vehicle you are likely to see is a pram, because this is a favourite walk for young families with small children. Very soon you pass a planked trail down to the river but it only leads to a not-very-exciting viewing point. Some 200 m further along a rough track leads down to the river and stepping stones. These in fact are huge slabs of concrete, very easy to walk across, but the river has flowed round the side and there are rough stones to cross there. But if the slabs aren't covered, it is well worth crossing, because on the south bank is a delightful path, soft underfoot, pleasanter and less frequented than the main track.

Follow this path through rather tangled forest to a footbridge across a side stream. Just beyond the bridge turn right on a path which takes you down to the river and the other 'stepping stones'. I use inverted commas because most of the concrete slabs have been tossed around by the floods or carried downstream and unless the water is pretty low it is not crossable. If you are serious about trying to cross back here I suggest boots and sticks are a good idea. Once across, a few steps bring you to the open area and the north bank track. However, even if you have to retrace your steps, it is a pleasant walk. Also, if you go just a little further you come into an open glade which makes a delightful picnic spot. You can explore beyond the glade, crossing a ruined wall to a sort of grotto of rounded boulders, but the path gets rougher and is hardly worth following. Along the path between the two sets of stepping stones, small tracks branch off towards the river, and especially if you have children with you there's plenty of diversion in following them.

Back at the lower stepping stones, re-cross the river to the main track. You can follow it back to the Centre, but it's more interesting to take the man-made trail with steps made of small logs, directly opposite the stepping stones. It takes you part way up the north side of the valley before curving round and bringing you back to the Centre.

If the river is uncrossable, continue along the main north bank track, which, even if not as attractive as the south bank, makes a pleasant stroll, again with the possibilities of narrow paths to be explored on both sides of the main track. Ten minutes or so brings you to an open space, with tracks leading off to left and right. That to the left leads to the upper stepping stones, that to the right climbs the slope to the edge of the wood. It may be possible to get out that way, but I am not sure if it is private property.

Retrace your steps to the lower stepping stones, and follow the man-made trail as described above back to the Centre. If you aren't picnicking, there are plenty of opportunities in Enniskerry to slake your thirst or get a bite to eat.

It is possible to do a longer walk but it is pretty rough in places and you definitely need Sheet 56. I can't really recommend it. Park as before or at the entry. Turn right along the main road towards the village, cross the bridge, pass the church and turn right uphill at the crossroads. The road climbs steeply out of the village and after about 1.5 km you turn very sharply right towards Glencullen. The road is then nearly straight for close on 2 km before it bears left and there is the Wood on your right — you will see the red boundary of the Conservation Area on the map. There's a stile, and beyond is a narrow track (marked on Sheet 56) down through the woods. It is narrow and side-sloping and just when you think you're there it rises over a buttress. This happens twice, but eventually you find yourself in the open glade of the south bank path. The whole round will probably take you a good 2½ hours. I had a complaisant chauffeur which saved the road walk but the path in the wood took longer than expected, especially as I lost the path.

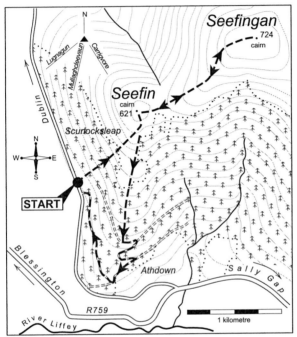

Distance: 4½ km
Ascent: 280 m
Time: 2 hours
Equipment: OSI Discovery Sheet 56. Boots, weather gear, sticks useful, compass if weather doubtful.

The equivalent of the Scottish 'Munros' (3,000 ft mountains) in Ireland are the 600 m mountains and Seefin is one of the handiest for Dublin peak-baggers. However, it is not just another summit to be ticked off; it has a wide view across the central plains and fine megalithic stone tomb on the summit. In fact it gets its name from the tomb, Suidhe Fionn, *Finn's seat or cairn (he seems to have as many tombs as Dermot and Grainne have beds!). For me it had the added interest that after many previous visits by various routes, while researching this guide I found not only a good (though rough!) new way up but a good new way down as well.*

From Dublin take the R114 through Rathfarnham and Old Bawn, past the Bohernabreena Reservoir entrance and up to the top of the hill beyond. At 'The Stone Cross' (but you won't see the fine granite cross until you've actually made the turn), fork left onto a narrow road signposted Kilbride. Drive along this road passing a firing range on the left and then a turn off on the right. About 1.3 km beyond the turn you will see a broad ride through the forest up the hill on your left. Park on the roadside (room for 3–4 cars). If this is crowded you can park a couple of hundred metres further along where a kissing gate gives entry to a surfaced forest road which is actually your return route.

Climb easily up the path in the ride until you emerge onto the open heathery hillside. Just here on the 1:50,000 map, in the typeface usually reserved for townlands is the name 'Scurlocksleap'. It is tempting to think of Scurlocks, with his black scurfy hair, making a mighty leap down the heather as he escapes from the pursuing soldiery. Back to our walk; follow a narrow, twisty, steep and rough path up through the heather beside a very aged fence until you meet the end of a broad track coming up through the forestry from the south. Note it — it's your return route. Bear left and a few metres beyond the track end, above a boulder heap, go left where the path forks and continue over a vaguer and vaguer path until the summit (621 m) and the tumulus are clear in front of you. The entrance (on the far side) has been dug out at some time in the past, but to my knowledge no serious archaeologist has investigated it. The lower, south-west side of the tumulus is generally sheltered from the wind so you can eat your sandwiches and enjoy the view in comfort. To the south-east, the main chain of the Wicklow Mountains marches south — Carrigvore, Gravale, Duff Hill buttress, Mullaghcleevaun, second highest mountain in Wicklow at 849 m. To its right is Black Hill (Walk 18) with its obvious track. Below you, south round to west is the Upper Liffey meandering round to the Pollaphuca Reservoir, which just appears as a bright gleam of water to the south-west over the top of Lugnagun (Walk 15). Beyond the Reservoir are the central plains, where the Liffey makes its big sweep west and north before turning back towards Dublin and the sea.

Blocking the view eastwards is 724 m Seefingan, also with a stone tumulus but a rather inferior one, and not on the actual summit — a cause of much frustration on a misty day. The reason why it, and other mountain tumuli are not at the actual summit is thought to be so that they can be seen from the valley if the summit is itself invisible from below. (Although it is the higher summit, the name sounds like a diminutive of Seefin — did the early surveyors mix up the names?) If you want to include it, the route is straight-forward and rather dull, just following the broad ridge into a slight dip and then climbing gently up the other side. If the cloud is down a compass (and the ability to use it) is definitely advisable. It will take you an extra hour.

If the cloud is down, indeed a compass is handy to set you off in the right direction from Seefin to pick up the vague path you mounted by. Fortunately no great map-reading knowledge is neces-sary; just head due south and in a couple of minutes you will find the path to bring you to the end of the broad track I asked you to note on the way up. I don't know the origin of this track or its purpose; the Coillte boundaries on the OSI map frame the upper part of it so perhaps it is an old right-of-way to the mountain commonage. Follow the track down through scattered forestry which gradually closes in on either side until you meet a forest road. Turn left along it and the rest is straightforward walking. The road zigs back to the right again (branch coming in on the left as you turn right), zigzags left and right and flattens out (another road in from the left). Go through (or over) a gate and keep round to the right (ignoring an exit onto the public road below) and continue along what could almost be called a forest highway (passing some fenced-off areas where broad-leaf saplings are being grown) to a huge turning circle and the kissing gate I mentioned at the beginning. Your car is either there, or visible up the road at the start. There isn't a watering hole nearby, but Blessington isn't too far away.

15. Lugnagun

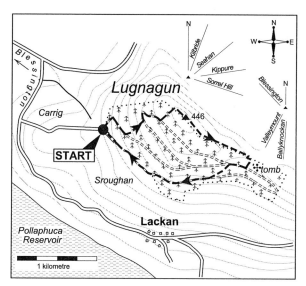

Distance: 4½ km
Ascent: 150 m
Time: 1½ hours
Equipment: OSI Discovery Series Sheet 56. Trainers (boots in winter), weather gear.

I'd never walked Lugnagun (Log na gcon, hollow of the hound) until I explored it for this walk and was pleasantly surprised — it is well worth a visit on a short winter's day or a summer's evening. There are several sections on forest roads but they are broken up by dashes through the woods and on the hilltop so they aren't long enough to be boring. The forest is mostly mature, with moss and pine needles underfoot. There are views over Pollaphuca, and finally, there is quite an interesting megalithic tomb to see.

Take the N81 to Blessington and turn left in the middle of the town (signposted Kilbride). Turn right over the bridge across the

Pollaphuca reservoir, and right again on the far side (signposted Lackan). Take the second turn left, a narrow road which leads you after a kilometre to a forest entrance on the left. Park there; space for about four cars.

Follow the broad forest road for about 12 minutes and then turn left into the trees. Alternate rows of trees have been felled so it is easy to pick an easy way straight up the hill between remaining rows. It is delightfully soft underfoot — mosses, club mosses and pine needles. As you climb you can see light ahead — the next road; when you reach it turn left and follow it round the corner and back eastwards, rising gently. (You could have followed forest roads to reach here, but it would have been longer — and duller.)

Some minutes along here the road is crossed by a ride. Turn left and climb the ride to the forest fence which has strategically placed stones to help you cross it. You are now on open heather hillside on the summit plateau of Lugnagun. Decide for yourself where the actual summit is — it doesn't rate a cairn. The view south unfortunately is blocked by the trees, but there's a view of the Liffey below Kilbride, backed by Seefin (Walk 14), Seefingan and Seahan. Be patient — there are better views further on.

A grassy path takes you along easily outside the bank that edges the forest, crossing a fence (more well-placed stones) to a break in the forest and the chance to look south and west across the reservoir and the plains beyond. Continue, dropping slowly, along the forest edge, until it begins to flatten out. Watch for a break in the bank and a stile in the forest fence. (If you get to a boggy bit at the source of a stream flowing north, you've gone a little too far.)

Now it gets interesting ... Cross the stile but don't follow the attractive-looking path downhill. Turn left and work your way amongst the trees to a ride, with a felled area beyond it. At this point you will mutter 'why didn't he tell me to cross the fence here?' and my answer is that the barbed wire fence is quite high with no stile or even useful stones. Keep along the fence for about 50 m, and if you look to your right you will see a cleared area and in it a small megalithic tomb. As I write, you can get right to it, but there are indications that it will be fenced off. When I first checked this walk, the tomb was hidden in the forest, and required detailed instructions and a map of its own to find it! There was even a tree growing out of the roof — now it seems Coillte appreciates its importance.

Return to the ride and follow it to a forest road. Turn right and in a couple of minutes you will see a ride diagonalling down to the left. Motor-cyclists have messed it up a bit but when I walked it there was a grassy track on one side. This brings you to a lower forest road on which you turn right and follow it to a barrier and a rough road outside the forest.

This leads back towards your parking place. After about ten minutes you meet new, hard, black tarmac (somebody must have influence!), and to turn you an envious green, below you nestling in the hillside are some fine houses, any of which I (and probably you) would love to own with the views from their windows across Pollaphuca to Valleymount and the hills beyond. Fortunately there's only about 5 minutes on the tarmac before you reach your transport.

The nearest pub is round to your left in Lackan, but Blessington with a wider choice is on your homeward route.

16. **Kilcoole Nature Reserve**

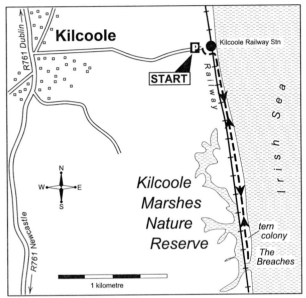

Distance: 4 km
Ascent: Negligible
Time: 1½–2 hours allowing for bird-watching
Equipment: OSI map Sheet 56. Trainers, rain gear, binoculars, bird and flower books.

*On the Wicklow coast below Kilcoole railway station there is a Nature Reserve which has many geese and other migrants in winter and in summer has a colony of breeding little terns. A sandy path beside the railway track gives easy access to the edge of the Nature Reserve with the bonus of a fine selection of flowers, including the pyramid orchid. It is a very pleasant evening stroll in summer and on a fine evening you won't be alone. In the winter it is an afternoon walk and often pretty breezy. I suggest you don't take a dog, but if you do, please **at least** keep it on a lead near the breeding colony. The simplest approach is to drive to the* *car park beside the station, but if you prefer public transport, buses pass the end of the road to the station. The railway isn't much help unfortunately because very few trains stop at the station. I have described the walk as an out-and-back, but you could continue to the next road inland and follow it to Newcastle and a bus. Check timetables!*

Take the N11 (Wexford road) from Dublin, past Kilmacanogue and through the Glen of the Downs, which is a glacial overflow channel with steep, wooded slopes rising nearly 200 m on either side. Just beyond the glen there is an exit left, signposted Delgany and (curiously!) Glenroe. This was the name of a very popular rural television soap opera, now defunct (perhaps the sign will have gone too). Go straight through Delgany village (signpost Greystones) and turn right at a large junction (signpost Kilcoole). In the middle of Kilcoole turn left and drive down to the railway station at the coast where there is a car park. A bus passes the end of the road to the railway station. Using it will add 3 km and about 45 minutes to your walk time.

Walk up to the level crossing and turn right. You pass a large rock inscribed to commemorate the landing of guns in 1914 from Conor O'Brien's yacht *Kelpie*, an exploit which has been largely overshadowed by the *Asgard* landing at Howth.

The path, which crosses to the sea-side of the railway line is rather sandy and a little tiring at first but it soon becomes grassier and more pleasant walking. In June, which is a very good time for the walk, you will find masses of yellow kidney vetch with, if you look carefully, purple pyramid orchids amongst them. Across the railway line is the Reserve and you should have your binoculars handy. There is meadowland, liable to flood, and grazing ground for many hundreds of geese in winter, and then more marshy ground with a long, branched, brackish lagoon, which on the map looks rather like a dragon. (See end for what birds you'll see and when.)

Don't neglect the view of the long waves rolling in with the long fetch from Wales; in fact in winter there are days when the spray from the breakers in an easterly gale will keep you very much aware of it!

In June, as you approach 'The Breaches', the outlet from the marsh to the sea, you will see a fenced-off area on the stony beach, the tern colony. This area is wardened and you will find a board with the tally of nests and hatched chicks. It is almost impossible to see the nests even with binoculars. All you can do is watch the crowd of little terns milling around above the beach, flying down to the sea to catch fish, and now and then dropping down to a nest — that's the moment when you may see a chick, practically invisible against the stones unless it moves.

You may wonder at the need for wardens and electric fencing; but I was talking to a warden who spent four nights watching for 'something' that had despoiled 15 nests of eggs, and eventually caught a hedgehog, which he then had to relocate a few miles away. Foxes also have to be guarded against.

The bridge beyond the colony at 'The Breaches' (but there is only one breach) is a good place to turn back if you are returning to Kilcoole. However, first admire the swirling tidal current as the large area of water in the lagoons fills or empties through the one narrow channel.

Return the same way, either to your car or to the bus. I can't recommend a pub in Kilcoole, but Delgany has both pleasant pubs and restaurants.

Some birds to watch out for:
(this is not a complete list)
Spring:
   Little gulls, some ducks and waders
Summer:
   Breeding little terns and ring plovers, a few swans and waders
Autumn:
   Early ducks and waders, including curlew, redshank, greenshank, dunlin
Winter:
   Whooper and Bewick's swans, brent- and grey-lag geese, wigeon, teal, and many waders

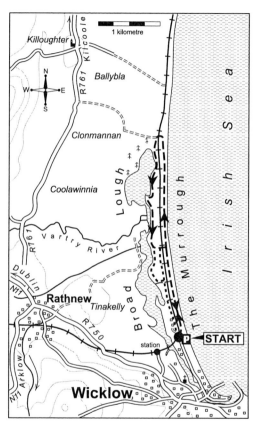

Distance: 6.3 km
Ascent: Negligible
Time: 1¾ to 2 hours for the basic route
Equipment: OSI Discovery Sheet 56. Trainers or walking shoes, rain gear, binoculars, bird book.

The Murrough is the shingle bank which forms the shore of the Irish Sea all the way from Greystones almost to Wicklow Harbour. The name

55

comes from the Irish murbhach, *meaning a salt marsh beside the sea, referring of course to the marsh and Broad Lough behind the shingle bank. When the ice retreated some 16,000 years ago, it left masses of sand and gravel deposited in the shallow basin which now forms the Irish Sea. This gravel was washed up to form a beach, and currents have moved the stones south along the shore. Look at the map and you will see that the Vartry River which once flowed straight out to sea was blocked by the gravel bank and now flows out to sea in Wicklow Harbour. As far as we are concerned the Murrough forms a pleasant, flat walking surface with good views out to sea, and Broad Lough is a fine place for bird-watching. Perhaps this isn't a walk for small children; the stretch along the Murrough is straight and rather dull, leading probably to boredom.*

Take the N11 (Wexford road) as far as Rathnew and fork left at the roundabout towards Wicklow town. Soon after passing under a railway bridge, turn left off the main road at a petrol station and follow a narrow, rather twisty road which leads you first uphill and then down to the river, and across a bridge. Turn left again onto a busy road leading to an industrial area. Pass one car park and continue along the road until, just before it crosses the railway line at a level crossing, there is another car park on the right, where you park. It is also possible to walk this route using the bus to Wicklow town. This will add at least half-an-hour to the walk.

The broad, level and grassy Murrough is just in front of you, beyond a low wall. Walk north along it, with the long straight vista of shoreline stretching away into the distance. You will probably not be alone; it is a great stretch for dog-walkers and also for elderly couples. (I checked it on a sunny weekday in late February, and it seemed everyone I met was at least as old as me!) Take a look at the large cobbles on the beach — they are all colours, demonstrating the varied strata of sandstone, limestone and conglomerates that the ice had collected in its travels. You may even notice granite, which has come all the way from Ailsa Craig off the coast of Ayrshire in Scotland.

You can tick off progress by noting the white posts which mark the quarter miles along the railway on your left, and before the 27-mile post you will see a gated crossing of the rails. (You will be coming back across the railway here on your return journey.) Continue along the Murrough, which is less used the further you get from Wicklow, so that in summer you may find a few flowers, such as yellow-horned poppy or sea sandwort.

You gradually approach some ruined houses and close to the first is another level crossing. Cross the line here (there's no pedestrian gate and last time I was there the big gate beyond the railway was locked and had to be climbed — but it isn't difficult!). Just in front of the ruined house turn left onto a broad low-level stretch of gravel between the gorse bushes beside the railway and a steep, high bank which separates you from the beds of reeds which close Broad Lough at this end. The stretch you are walking was a gravel pit in the 1980s, but extraction has fortunately now been stopped. After a few minutes walk, the excavated area finishes and you can easily climb onto the high level to your right, whence a narrow path will lead you down to the shore of Broad Lough. (If by any chance you reverse this walk, leave Broad Lough and head over to the gravel pit just before the wreck of a small, pale-blue rowing boat.)

Your route turns left, but if you want to see some reed birds, it is worth following the path right to the head of the Lough where, in the extensive reed beds, you may see reed buntings, sedge warblers, and occasionally reed warblers or bearded tits. Return to the wreck of the rowing boat.

The walk down the Lough follows a narrow and occasionally rather rough path along the shore (the prevailing west and southwest winds deposit much flotsam on this eastern shore). Now is the moment to keep your bird book and binoculars handy. In winter Broad Lough shelters large flocks of mute swans, wigeon, teal and many species of wader, including curlews and lapwings. In autumn migrating swallows and martins pass through. As for predators, kestrels hunt over the grasslands and hen harriers may be seen over the reeds in winter.

The Lough narrows and a broad promontory of marsh projects into it. A little further south, a good eye can distinguish the mouths of the two branches of the Vartry River on the east shore. As I mentioned in the Introduction, the river used to flow directly to the sea here, but has been diverted by the moving shingle of the Murrough south to Wicklow Harbour.

The Lough begins to broaden again, and opposite some renovated stables there is a good path heading towards the sea. Follow this back across the railway line by the crossing near milestone 27 and return to your car by your outward route. It is also possible to continue further south along the shore to a stone wall. Turn left along a path which leads back to the railway line. You can turn right along a road which leads past the port storage area and other industrial buildings back to your car. It is not recommended unless you are short of time — the road is hard, muddy and busy. Better to turn left and follow the path to the rail crossing.

Wicklow town offers plenty of opportunities to eat and drink.

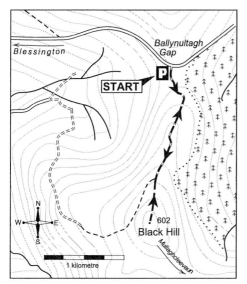

Distance: 4 km
Ascent: 160 m
Time: 1¼ to 1½ hours
Equipment: OSI Discovery Sheet 56 or Harvey Map. Boots, weather gear, compass, sticks useful.

Black Hill, on the normal route up Mullaghcleevaun from the west, is a nice little walk in its own right. The road over the saddle between Sorrel Hill and Black Hill takes you to 445 m, leaving you a mere 160 m to get to a fine viewpoint, ranging from Kippure in the north to the top of Lugnaquilla in the south. There's a track most of the way, but while it starts well it gets very stony, and also has boggy patches, hence the recommendation of boots and, if you don't like rough going, sticks. The summit is very rounded and if the mist comes down, you really do need a compass to start you walking down in the right direction. We checked it out on a glorious sunny, breezy spring morning, but it would be equally attractive on a summer's evening, with the sun setting over the midland plains. If you are a collector of 600 m summits, then Black Hill just squeezes in at 602 m.

The approach is the same as Lugnagun (Walk 15) but having crossed the reservoir, instead of turning off the Lackan road for Lugnagun, continue through Lackan village, where you fork left and climb to the car park on the saddle.

The track is obvious, heading towards the rounded summit, winding through the heather. It is an old bog road, and higher up you will find plenty of old turf cuttings. As you mount the track deteriorates until you are simply picking your way amongst small, rounded granite boulders lying on coarse granite sand. The summit looks very near but it is only the first of several false tops. The path disappears under rough bog and heather cover, which has served to stop the four-wheel-drive quads. Note on your right a group of distinctive large, sharp-edged boulders — they are a good landmark to head for on your way down. Beyond the boulders there is really no path but the heather is shorter and soon replaced by grass so that walking is easy until you reach the diminutive moated summit cairn which hardly projects above the surrounding surface.

Now for the view. Clockwise from the north-west, Lugnagun (Walk 15) and Sorrel are easy to recognise, then Seefin and Seefingan (Walk 14), easily picked out by their prehistoric cairns, and Kippure with its mast. Next the summit of Maulin just peeps out and then to the east is the main chain of the Wicklow Mountains from Carrigvore over majestic Mullaghcleevaun to Tonelagee and the flat top and water tower of Turlough Hill. Further away to the south is the Lugnaquilla ridge and much nearer is Moanbane, separated from the Mullagh by Billy Byrne's Gap, which Art O'Neill probably crossed on his escape from Dublin Castle in 1592, only to die in the snow at the head of Glenreemore. It's worth wandering around a bit on this flat summit to see down to the valley on the east, where you'll find the beautifully named Loughnavreen Banks, and to the west the Pollaphuca lake, Ballyknockan, the 'Granite Village' of the quarrymen (Walk 21), the bridge and arc of land that leads to Valleymount, and the midland plains beyond.

Now it is time to return. My companion on the checking visit who lives nearby and lopes her way over all these hills was very firm that really there is no other reasonable way down except the upward route, so you should head back to the north, keeping an eye out for the boulders so you can pick up the track back to the your car.

There's a pub in Lackan, or a wider choice in Blessington.

Djouce Mountain

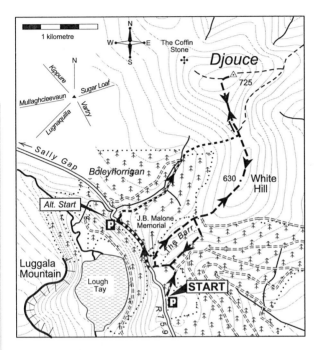

Distance: 8 km

Ascent: 275 m

Time: 2¾ hours

Equipment: OSI Discovery Sheet 56. Boots (winter), trainers (summer), weather gear. Sticks useful for the alternative route. Compass useful for alternative ascent in cloud.

This is probably the easiest mountain of its size in Wicklow to climb. Its summit is near the section of the Wicklow Way which, because of boggy ground and heavy use, now has a sleeper track laid at enormous cost. Where there isn't a sleeper track there is a good path. But don't scorn it because of its ease. There is the J.B. Malone Memorial to see, with great views down Lough Tay and Lough Dan and away over ridges getting bluer and fainter in the distance to Lugnaquilla, Leinster's highest mountain. Just don't pick a holiday weekend or you'll be jostled off the sleeper track by Wicklow Way walkers, or worse, by mountain bikers. If you can't face the sleeper track both ways, I can offer an alternative.

Checking for this guide I was up Djouce on a cold, sunny, January day; there wasn't a breath of wind and Lough Tay was like glass — may you be as lucky.

Take the N11 to Kilmacanogue and turn right onto the R755. After about 11 km turn right onto the R759 (signposted Sally Gap). The road climbs the hill and emerges into the open above Lough Tay. Follow the road high above the Lough until you come to a large car parking area on the right side of the road, with a Wicklow Way yellow man marker pointing into it. Park there. (If you are starting from West Dublin the quicker approach would be over the Featherbed to the Sally Gap crossroads, where you turn left and approach the Wicklow Way car park from the other direction.)

Follow the Wicklow Way into the forest and go left over a stile at the first junction. Then go left again at a Y-junction (the other branch is the way you will descend) and follow a gravel path through the trees onto the hillside. Almost immediately you come upon the sleeper walkway, bearing round to the right. A couple of minutes up the walkway brings you to a large boulder with a memorial stone to J.B. Malone at its foot. 'JB' was one of the great pioneers of Irish hillwalking. His weekly articles in the *Evening Herald*, spanning more than 30 years, probably brought more Dubliners onto the hills than any other factor. In later years, as Field Officer of the Long Distance Walking Routes Committee, he was able to fulfil his long-cherished dream of a waymarked walk through the Wicklow Mountains. As mentioned, above his memorial site offers a wonderful view down to Lough Tay and beyond.

Continue along the sleeper track which here winds its way across the bog, offering pleasant walking instead of a mucky trudge. The sleepers have been set with some clearance between them and the ground to permit regeneration of the natural flora — heather, bog cotton and sphagnum moss. It is a pity to 'civilise' this mountain bogland, but heavy use was creating a wider and wider area without vegetation cover as walkers moved out to one side or the

Djouce Mountain

other to keep clear of the morass.

The sleeper track drops down to a fence with a stile and then climbs to the vague, rounded summit of White Hill. Now as you follow the track into the shallow gap between White Hill and Djouce the view to the east opens out, with the Vartry reservoirs prominent. Beyond the gap, as you climb gently, the Wicklow Way and its sleeper track swings off the ridge to the east, while you continue up a clear, broad path which leads you to within sight of the tors which mark the summit of Djouce Mountain, 725 m. A little unexpectedly they turn out to be of mica schist, the metamorphic rock which originally overlaid the dome of Wicklow granite. A further view opens up from the Great Sugar Loaf in the north-east swinging across Glensoulan to Maulin, Tonduff, Kippure and round to the hills beyond the Military Road. Its situation east of the backbone of the Wicklow Mountains makes Djouce a fine viewpoint.

The return, to start with anyhow, is by the same path. It's no problem to find the path in clear weather, but if it's misty, take care on the way up to note small ground indications by which you can pick up the path on your return.

By the time you have followed the sleeper track back as far as the fence, you'll be feeling like the traditional hen following a chalk line; so as soon as you've crossed the fence, turn left and follow a good path which leads over a stile (a little rickety) into the forest. Turn right along a forest track which takes you in a switchback (rather wet in the two hollows I'm afraid) back to your outward route at the start of the gravel path under the trees. Turn left and follow the outward route back to the car park.

Alternative. If you don't want to go both ways along the sleeper track, there is another route you can take. Timewise it's about the same, but it is definitely rougher — sticks might be handy. Instead of parking at the Wicklow Way car park, continue to the forest entrance just before Boleyhorrigan Bridge and park there. Follow the forest road through the wood (felled on one side) to where it ends. Climb straight ahead towards the open hillside and Djouce ahead. It looks alarmingly rough with branches strewn everywhere, but once you've crossed two small streams, the rest of the way to the open hillside is quite easy. Once in the open you will see, straight ahead, a narrow path winding through the heather beside a re-entrant, which you should follow until it disappears. Now you can head direct for the summit of Djouce, but I suggest that it is less steep to head through quite deep heather for the flat saddle between Djouce and White Hill (if it is misty the compass bearing is approximately 35° Magnetic). You should reach the saddle and join the main route roughly where the Wicklow Way swings off down to the right. Climb the path to the summit, admire the view (see above) and return along the upward track of the main route until, after passing the J.B. Malone Memorial, the sleeper track forks. Take the right fork which descends along the forest edge, and then bears right down to the road. Turn right and follow the road for a little less than a kilometre back to your car.

If you have a few minutes to spare, I suggest you visit the superb belvedere which overlooks Lough Tay, with its sandy beach and the great Luggala crag frowning over it. You reach it by a narrow path to the right leading off the road a short distance south of the Wicklow Way car park, at the crown of the hill.

The nearest source of refreshment is Roundwood village, where there's a variety of pubs and eating places.

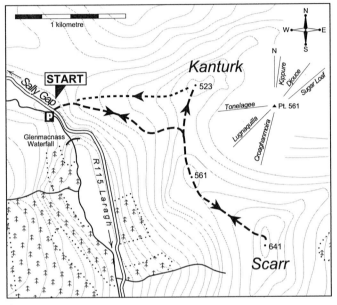

Distance: 5 km
Ascent: 290 m
Time: 2 hours (add 15 minutes for Kanturk Mountain)
Equipment: OSI Discovery Sheet 56 or Harvey Map. Boots, weather gear, compass if the cloud is down.

It is often true that outlying mountains not on the main chain of a range offer the best views, and of course they have the advantage that they are easier to climb. I picked Scarr (Sceir, sharp rock) for both these reasons. It is, except for a couple of short, steep sections, a gently graded walk over heather and tussocky grass. There are bilberries too, and if you time your walk for July, you can have a feast on the way. I selected the route from the car park above the Glenmacnass waterfall because there is less ascent, and because there is a car park — the alternative route from the Lough Dan side has parking difficulties at time of writing. Of course if you can find a pliant car driver who will drop you at Lough Dan and pick you up at the waterfall then you could have an almost perfect walk.

My preferred approach is by the N11 to Kilmacanogue where you turn off onto the R755 to Laragh, and fork right onto the R115 up Glenmacnass. This is part of the Military Road built around 1800 to flush out the survivors of the 1798 Rising who were still holding out in the Wicklow Mountains. It is a pleasant winding road, much of it through trees and after a few minutes the fine Glenmacnass waterfall comes in view, a magnificent sight after heavy rain. The road climbs up beside the waterfall to the car park above it. (You may be astonished at the rash of warning signs. They arise from an accident some years ago when a man slipped, fell down the waterfall and was killed. The court held there were insufficient warning signs and the farmer who owns the waterfall is taking care there should not be another tragedy.) In the car park make sure your handbrake is fully on — years ago I saw a parked car slowly gather speed of its own volition, climb over the bank and slide gently into the river, more or less undamaged. The baby in his cot had been removed from the car only a minute or two before. Hardly believably, the tractor that came to tow the car out did exactly the same thing, and a bulldozer had to be found to pull them both out!

Across the road from the car park a rather vague little path takes you up the first steep hillside only to fade away where the slope eases. Now you must slant to your right, utilising some of the many sheep tracks which cross the slope. Soon you can see the ridge and when the sheep tracks die out, head towards a slight bump in the level ridge on the near side of an obvious rocky summit. Once on the ridge you find a broad track which brings you to the rise to the rocky summit. As you climb it, you will notice the change in rock. The grey granite is gone, replaced by smooth slaty rock which almost appears to glint with some kind of ore. No, it isn't an outcrop of the fabled Wicklow gold, just the shine in the sunlight of the mica in the metamorphic schist which once covered all the Wicklow granite and now only remains as capping for some of the hills. Another disappointment awaits you — this isn't the summit of Scarr. A further trudge along a ridge and another climb are needed to bring you to the true summit.

But pause here, because the views are better. Far away to the north-west is the Great Sugar Loaf's obvious pyramid; swinging anti-clockwise, Djouce (Walk 19), War Hill, Kippure with its mast and the main chain of the Wicklow Mountains right down to Lugnaquilla are all visible. Finally, to the south-east, another pyramid, Croaghanmoira (Walk 32) completes the view.

Continue to the summit (641 m) — it is 15 minutes walking along a broad, breezy, easy ridge with a short climb at the end onto the narrow summit ridge. There are convenient nooks where you can lunch out of the wind and either look down on Glenmacnass or on the alternative route from Lough Dan.

Return the way you came, over the rocky summit and down to an upright stone on the level ridge. Here you have a choice; either reverse your upward route or continue to Kanturk, 529 m (*Ceann tuirc*, wild boar peak). (Walkers generally prefer the alternative name, Brown Mountain, a name which the Harvey Map has moved to the lower summit to the east, without, as far as I know, any justification.)

If reversing, diagonal downhill, aiming for the north end of the wood that backs the car park. To be honest, it will probably be by chance that you hit your upward path from the car park and if in doubt keep further on where there is a gentler slope to the road. For Kanturk, continue along the ridge to its rather indistinct and marshy summit and then turn left down the broad ridge which leads you back to the road and car park. If visibility is very bad a compass might be useful in descent from Kanturk; Magnetic west will take you back to your car.

Returning to Dublin, if you want a change from your outward drive, continue north along the winding Military Road, right through the middle of the mountains, past Sally Gap crossroads and down to Rathfarnham. (This might be a better approach route for people living in West Dublin.) I brought you via Laragh for a view of the waterfall, and if you want food or drink you'll have to go back to Laragh!

21.   Ballyknockan —
Stonecutters' Village

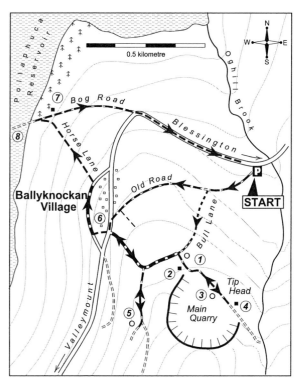

Distance: 2½ km
Ascent: 80 m
Time: 1 hour plus viewing time!
Equipment: OSI Discovery Sheet 56, *Ballyknockan* book (see below).
Walking shoes or trainers, rain gear.

The granite quarries of Ballyknockan village, overlooking Blessington Lake, are the source from which much of the stone of Dublin's buildings was drawn. Nearly everything in Ballyknockan is made of granite, the cottages have ashlar granite porches and even the fence posts are granite!

It is a wonderful place to visit, and I just had to include it in this book. If possible, try to get hold of Ballyknockan — A Wicklow Stonecutters' Village *by Séamas Ó Maitiú and Barry O'Reilly, The Woodfield Press. I'm told it is still in print though it is hard to find; it should be available in public libraries. It is a full history of the village, with maps, drawings and photographs and tells you far more than I have space for. I am indebted to it for much of the information below.*

I am afraid there is quite a lot of tarmac walking, but there are so many sights to see that I think you will hardly notice the hardness of the road. I mention some of the outstanding features in granite, but really there is something to see in nearly every house. The whole area is littered with abandoned blocks of granite, some part-worked, others just rough. There are still many stoneworkers working in the village, mainly I think on funeral monuments. Debris is inevitable in any quarry area, but otherwise the village is very tidy and well-preserved, with neat white-on-black polished granite labels for each road or lane.

Approach from Dublin as for Walk 18 (Black Hill), but in Lackan village fork right and follow the road round the lake for about 4 km to a bridge and a car park on the left, where you should leave your car. Walk up the track (this is the old road) towards the village. After about 100 m you will see on your left a narrow grassy track between two high granite walls ('Bull Lane'). At the time of writing this is quite overgrown but by the time you read this I expect it to be cleared. If it is easily walkable (*please* don't try to force your way through), follow it until it opens out and you see a gate ahead. Go through the gate and follow a track to a tarmac road, where you join the route we had to follow when checking the walk.

If the Lane is not easily walkable, continue along the track which joins the new tarmac road through the village. Follow it until you see a road going up the hill with a signpost to McEvoy's Monumental Works. Walk up this road, bear left at a junction with a track and you soon see a track coming in your left with the name-plate 'Bull Lane'; this is where the two approaches join. Continue up the road and almost immediately you see a rough sculptured lion (1) on your left. This was one of a 'pride' ordered for the entrance avenue to Stormont, Belfast, but (according to Belfast) rejected because the rough cut did not leave enough provision for the final carving. However, Ballyknockan said that the Belfast masons, used to Mourne's granite, couldn't work the harder Wicklow granite and that eventually some Ballyknockan masons had to go to Belfast! The large, round stone beside the lion was used for shaping the iron tyres of the carts which carried the stone to Dublin. Opposite is the fine Granite House (2) with a sumptuously ornate granite door surround.

Continue up the road to an open area from which you can look into the main quarry on your right. There will probably not be any actual quarrying in progress but on a weekday you will almost certainly hear hammer-tapping as a stone-cutter works on some new commission. There is a high working face, easily recognisable by the vertical drill holes. There are two big cranes, one of them an old-style derrick, something rarely seen any longer. There's a modern stone cross (3) to commemorate quarrymen of past generations. Now turn your back on the quarry to look at the view. The whole north end of the Lake is before you, from Lackan round to Blessington. The OSI Discovery map suggests a viewpoint at the car park, but thanks to the extra height, there's a far better view from here.

This is as far as you can go, but before turning back take a look at Granite Cottage (4) with its fine ashlar porch. Return past the lion and where the tarmac turns downhill keep going straight along a track which quickly brings you to a beautiful Madonna and Child (5). It was rejected because the Child was held in Our Lady's right arm rather than her left. It is a sensitive piece of carving, the Madonna looking tenderly down, her head cowled and her cloak flowing in a simple curve. How foolish it was to reject it, but we are the gainers — don't miss it!

Return to the tarmac and descend to the main road. Almost immediately opposite is a narrow path — 'The Black Lane' (6) which leads you past the ruin of a fine house with an ashlar chimney stack, into the centre of the village. Turn right to pass the Ballyknockan Inn and the old cinema/dance hall, a barn now being converted into apartments. This has been done reasonably sensitively, but there is rather too much polished granite, which is not in keeping with the older buildings. Turn left beyond this building and walk down a narrow, sunken lane between high stone walls of massive granite blocks — this is 'The Horse Lane' which joins a broad track near the Lake. This track — 'The Bog Road' — was the route by which the carts used to bring the stone to Dublin. Now it ends abruptly on the shore of the Lake; before the flooding in 1940 it was the road to Valleymount (8). Your curiosity will probably be aroused by the gable end in the field beside the track with the inscription 'The Emergency Land-grabber defeated here 1888 — God Save Ireland'. The story goes that a local man bought the land, evicted an old woman living there and demolished her cottage. Local people rebuilt it in a night, but the 'grabber' demolished it again, nearly killing the owner. However, she eventually went to court, got the land back, and the local people rebuilt the house again! It is known as the 'Land League House' (7).

There's a gate at the end of the track with some fierce notices of the ESB, but they seem to be generally disregarded, and you might be brave enough to walk the path through the wood bordering the Lake, past a couple of moored yachts into a very pleasant conifer grove, exactly the place for a picnic.

Now all that's left is to follow the Bog Road to its junction with the main road, and walk the main road back to your car. You may, no doubt, have already marked out one or other of the village pubs for a visit.

For your journey home, I suggest you continue to Valleymount to admire the parish church of the Ballyknockan stonecutters, with its granite pinnacles. From Valleymount it is straightforward to return to Blessington, and it is only about 4 km longer than the Lackan route.

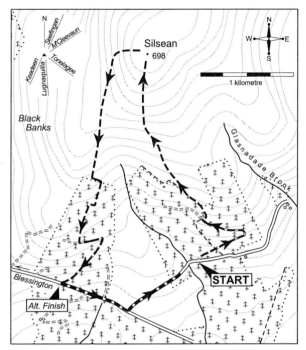

Distance: 6.8 km
Ascent: 350 m
Time: 2¾ hours
Equipment: OSI Discovery Sheet 56 (Harvey Map useful for start). Boots, weather gear, sticks advised, compass if any doubt about the weather.

Silsean (suillseán, a place of lights?) is the last mountain on the ridge bounding Glen Bride on the west. It can't be said to be an exciting summit. It is marked by a single wooden post on the level summit plateau and one wonders how the surveyors decided that was the actual high point — if indeed it is. But it is one of the higher mountains in Wicklow, is not very difficult to climb and like many outliers, gives some fine views all round. Coillte provides handy routes between road and mountainside,

73

both in ascent and descent, and one section of the descent is truly beautiful — not an adjective often used of conifer plantations! I have suggested a compass because the summit plateau is so featureless that it would be very easy to descend in the wrong direction if the visibility is poor. It is a fair weather walk anyway, the view is an important part of its attraction. On the mountainside the ground is not very rough, but don't expect to find a path!

From Dublin take the N11 and beyond Blessington, turn left onto the R758, signposted Valleymount. Having passed Valleymount, at the second junction fork left, a narrow road (not the place to meet a tractor) which rises over a spur of Silsean and then descends gently through forest. (If in doubt, follow the St Kevin's Way signs, on which the familiar yellow walking man has been replaced by a cheerful-looking yellow pilgrim.) There are two forest entrances on the left of this road, and the second is where you emerge on the way down from the mountain. If you want to avoid the 1.5 km road walk back to your car, you could leave a second car here. Anyway, for the start continue downhill and (leaving the yellow pilgrim) turn left along another narrow road for about 0.8 km to a forest entrance below a huge felled area of forest. Park there.

It is here that the Harvey Map is useful; it shows the forest road and track I describe below clearly and accurately, unlike the OSI which omits the forest road. OSI also shows a band of trees reaching right up to the summit of Silsean. It doesn't exist, and I can only suppose that the Forest Service bought the land many years ago but never planted it — I don't think that Coillte would now consider planting at such a height.

Walk up the forest road which rises gently. Soon you come to a junction and a track rising steeply to the left. When we were checking, it was full of brashings, and the obvious route was to continue along the forest road which zigs back to cross the track again higher up. At this second junction you must turn right up the track, which very soon becomes clear of brashings. It is paved with cobbles which make easy walking and is obviously the old road up to the peat cuttings visible on the mountain side above the forestry. It climbs gently, curves round to the left and leaves Coillte property at a wooden gate. Continue along the track until you come to what might pass for a stony turning circle just before the track degenerates and bends down to the left.

Abandon the track at the turning circle and climb straight up the hillside to the rounded top of Silsean. It is easy going, over low heather and tough grass. We were there checking in mid-May 2003, and there still wasn't a bite for a hungry sheep. It is just a matter of plodding determinedly up the slope which gets steeper and rougher as you rise. However, the surface is fairly dry and though there are three false crests to disappoint you, eventually you reach that single timber post.

Ahead the broad ridge continues to Moanbane, but it hardly interferes with the panoramic view of the Wicklow Mountains. To the north is Seefingan (Walk 14) easily identifiable by its cairn, and Kippure (equally easily recognisable by its mast!). Nearer at hand, towards the east, Mullaghcleevaun with its sharp prow masks the main backbone to its north, but south of it Tonelagee stands out clearly with the Camaderry reservoir to its right. Due south Lugnaquilla peers over the nearer hills, and away to the south-west the isolated Keadeen is easily seen. However, for the view over Blessington Lake Reservoir and the midlands, you must walk 100 m or so westwards to the brow of the plateau. There you will find as good a view of the Lake as you can find anywhere with all its bays and inlets and especially the long cape projecting north from Valleymount, looking like a monstrous snake's head.

A second reason for going a little west is that you can see a big plantation to the south, left of the south-west ridge — it is not visible from the summit. In case you get caught by mist the compass bearing is about 215° Magnetic. All you have to do now is head down the slope towards the forest, more or less parallel with the Lake. As you descend the slope flattens out and you walk on almost bare turf — there was a heath fire some years ago and there has been very little regrowth. Be a little careful, there are some holes and caves in the peat.

Getting into the forest provides the only navigational problem — and it is not really a difficult one. The start of the path through it, not easily seen from a distance, is about the middle of the top edge of the forest. It is best to aim a little to the west (right) of the middle and walk down beside the forest edge. You pass a sort of cock's comb of tall grass and come to four fence posts quite close together. There your path through the wood starts; it is also distinguishable by the remains of an old netting fence going down beside you into the forest.

A short distance into the forest the trees arch over you. A pale green moss coats the branches and also hangs from them in trails. It is delicately beautiful and very eerie; one almost expects to see fairies flitting amongst the trees. This pale green corridor continues for some distance and then the path emerges into a wide gap between two forested areas. It is fenced off and one can only surmise that some obstinate landowner refused to sell his strip of land. The going is very rough for a short distance — gullies crossing the strip have to be negotiated. But soon a faint path appears on the left (lower) side of the strip and your troubles are over. Continue along this path, which becomes gradually clearer as you approach a forest road. The open strip continues beyond the road, but it is fenced off so it is preferable to follow the forest road to the left. After one zig it brings you to the public road, as noted in the approach to the start. Unless you have left a car here, turn left and follow the public road back to the start.

You can rehydrate in Valleymount, or perhaps more interestingly, turn right before Valleymount and go to Ballyknockan, some 2 km along the road. There's a pleasant pub and there is added interest that this is the village where much of Dublin's granite masonry was quarried (see also Walk 21). Refreshed, you can continue north along the Lake shore through Lackan and back to Blessington.

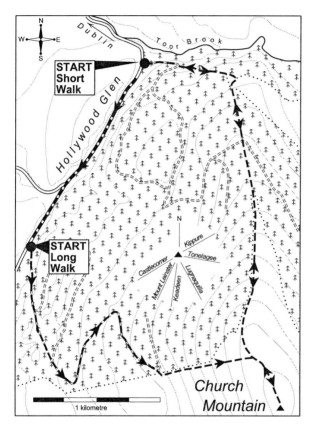

Distance: (long) 7.2 km; (short) 5.6 km

Ascent: 360 m

Time: (long) 3 hours; (short) 2¼–2½ hours

Equipment: OSI Discovery Sheet 56. Boots, weather gear, compass if the cloud is down.

Church Mountain is an isolated summit offering wonderful views, north over Pollaphuca Reservoir and the King's River valley, south and west over the central plains and distant Mount Leinster. I am suggesting two walks here. The longer walk has considerable advantages; there is better parking, it is a circular walk, and it takes you through the Hollywood Glen, a spectacular glacial overflow channel cut through the hill. On the other hand, the upper part of the climb is very steep and quite rough. The shorter walk, actually up and back along the descent route of the longer walk, saves at least half-an-hour, is not so steep but is less varied.

Church Mountain got its name because it is supposed to be the site of a chapel built by St Palladius, who came to Ireland long before St Patrick. (I am indebted to J.B. Malone's Walking in Wicklow *for information about the summit of the mountain.)*

Take the N81 out of Dublin, through Blessington and past Pollaphuca. Look out for the junction left signed Hollywood and Glendalough, but continue and turn left at the next (very minor) junction. Pass a road to the left, and follow your road round a sharp left turn (old limekiln just to your right) and along beside the Toor Brook to a sharp right turn and almost immediately a forest entrance. This is the start of the shorter walk (parking for two cars). For the longer walk continue straight through the Glen to another forest entrance, the start of the walk, with parking for at least half-a-dozen cars.

Take the forest road leading up right and follow it on a long sweep to the south, ignoring two roads leading off left. The wood is particularly pleasant, plenty of open ground, mature trees, little hills and valleys, small crags half-seen through the trees. The road swings round left in a long rise north-east and then back south-east to a gate at the forest edge where the road bends back north.

Go through the gate which opens onto a hillside planted with young trees; turn left and climb steeply up a rough path beside the old wood. After about 100 m of ascent the forest diverges away to the left, but you should continue straight up beside the straggly fence until the slope eases and the fence turns left. Almost immediately you meet a good track. Turn right along this and follow it for a short distance until it comes close to another fence. Almost opposite, a narrow ill-defined path leads across a gentle tussocky grass slope towards the summit cairn which is clearly visible. If you miss this path, it doesn't matter too much, but it is easier walking than the tussocks.

The summit boasts a huge stone cairn in the form of a ring of jumbled granite stones and if you search diligently you might find some worked stones and stumps of wall (of St Palladius' chapel?). There is also, according to 'JB', a holy well in a hollow in the middle of the cairn but we didn't see it. There were 'patterns' up here a century ago, so this has certainly been a holy mountain, pagan or christian, for several millennia.

If you stand on the highest heap of stones there is a wonderful full circle view. South-west beyond the Barrow are the Castlecomer Hills, almost due south is Mount Leinster. Closer at hand is Brusselstown Ring and to its left Keadeen rises sharply. Lugnaquilla's North Prison can be seen above the nearer Lobawn and Imaal Sugar Loaf, while across the King's River Valley north of the Wicklow Gap are Tonelagee, Mullaghcleevaun and in the distance Kippure with its television mast. So from this one viewpoint you can see the five highest mountains in Leinster! Before you descend look north to the peaceable lowlands around the Pollaphuca reservoir with its two main branches spanned by the bridges at Blessington and Valleymount.

Now for the descent. From the flat, round summit plateau it takes a little thought to pick up the vague little path by which you ascended, and if the cloud is down a compass might be useful. Heading a little west of north will bring you to the path and back to the fence and your upward track. Reverse this but remain on it as it swings round right and crosses the fence. A sufficiency of stones has been piled against the fence to make it fairly easy to cross. Continue along the track beside the fence, descending to the north across open moorland. This track, by the way, is an old turf road from the turf cuttings east of Church Mountain.

Soon you meet the forest edge, but the track continues straight down, more steeply, as a clear ride between two forest blocks. The slope eases a bit and you cross a forest road, gated on the left and climbing gently to the right. Continue on and the forest ends soon on your right. Use the large boulder to cross a fence and immediately turn left to cross a second one. Follow this down past an old walled enclosure until you meet a track through the trees. Turn left along this sunken track and it will lead you to open ground and a sharp corner in a forest road. Go downhill along this road which in a very few minutes brings you out on the public road at the point I mentioned as the start of the shorter route.

Turn left and walk the public road, the original post road to Donard and south, between the dramatic steep sides of the Glen. The east side is heavily wooded, the west is more open, with a row of crags. The OSI map shows a hillfort on the top of the ridge, but I wouldn't fancy climbing to it, certainly not as an enemy! Twenty minutes along the road should bring you back to your car.

For the shorter walk, park as already explained, and follow the descent route in reverse. Be careful in a few places where you might miss the route. At the sharp bend in the forest road soon after the start, there are two grassy paths nearly straight ahead — take the right-hand one, the other just goes down to the Toor Brook. Where your path comes into the open, you must turn sharply right, keeping the enclosure wall on your left to pick up the long straight ride through the forest. Where you meet the forest road (gate on your right), don't be beguiled by the road rising gently on your left — it is a dead end! Continue straight up the ride, which steepens and is definitely boring, so it is great to suddenly come out on the open hillside above. The rest of the way to the summit is adequately described in the descent route.

If you feel, as you may well do, the need for refreshment, go back to Hollywood (you may have noticed the signpost on the way out) and pick one of the two pubs, opposite each other in the middle of the village. Hollywood is the start of St Kevin's Way, the path he is supposed to have followed to Glendalough. It was followed by many pilgrims and has now been turned into a way-marked Pilgrim Path sponsored by the Heritage Council. Unfortunately a lot of it is on road but, restored by your pub visit you should certainly follow it for a few hundred metres from the village to a pleasing little ice-cut valley containing St Kevin's Statue, his Cave and his Seat — and the Norman motte of Hollywood.

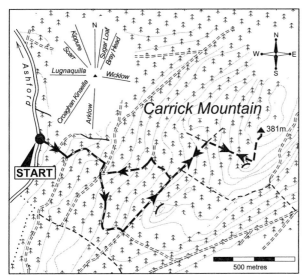

Distance: 5 km
Ascent: 180 m
Time: 1¾ hours
Equipment: OSI Discovery Sheet 56. Boots (winter), runners (summer), weather gear, sticks useful.

Fifty years ago I remember enjoying a great scramble along over the granite tors that form the backbone of Carrick Mountain. However, it wasn't long after that the Forestry Service bought up the mountain and planted most of it, leaving only the rocky pimples projecting from the dark green forest. I'd more or less given up the idea of finding a walk there, and certainly the first route that a friend and I found to the top couldn't possibly be described as an easy walk. But we persevered, and — yes, there is a quite easy walk to the summit and a wide-ranging view. Basically, it is up and down the same way, but if you want extra exercise it is quite easy to find it on the forest tracks. Just don't get lost like the babes in the wood.

Take the N11 from Dublin to Ashford and turn right at the round-about at the entrance to the village. Keep left at three successive junctions (the third is signposted Rathdrum). Follow the rather twisty road (passing one crossroads) for about 4 km to a second crossroads; turn left and after about 1.2 km there is a forest entrance on your left, where you should park (if you come to a road junction with a road on to the right, you've gone too far!).

Walk the forest road through a felled area with young trees to a junction where you fork left and start climbing, quite gently. The next junction has five tracks; take the third which rises more steeply through a fine mature wood. This brings you nearly to the crest of the ridge and another junction where you turn left along a contour-ing track below the ridge, past a magnificent steep rocky tor, steep enough to deter Coillte from planting it. Continue along the track, dipping a little, with wood on the right and some open ground on the left, passing a track on the right and rising again to another junction where you should follow a rather rough path that heads straight up the hill on the right. As you climb there is a mature stand of spruce on your left, presumably saved from felling to give some protection to the birch trees planted beyond. Soon you emerge from the trees and suddenly you are in a different world. The path improves and turns left along the ridge crest beside another tor. There are trees on the slopes on either side but ahead are boulder-strewn slopes of heather leading towards the summit cairn. Though the main path stops, a twisty path through the heather takes you the last few metres to the cairn.

You are above the trees and Carrick is an isolated hill so there are fine views, away south to Arklow and the Wexford coast, round to distant Croaghan Kinsella, Croaghanmoira (Walk 32), Lugnaquilla and the main Wicklow range. All this from a summit of only 381 m.

The twisty path continues east, tempting the walker to follow it to the next tor, but, sadly, it soon loses itself in a thick belt of spruce. So the only alternative is to return the way you came. When you have reached the contouring track, however, instead of continuing right the way along it there are possible alternatives.

If you feel the need for more exercise, turn up the hill at the next junction, following a track which climbs over the ridge crest and contours along below a tor to a T-junction. Go down the hill to a major junction, and turn right onto a good contouring forest road. Fork right at the first junction, continuing to contour, and right again to cross the ridge to rejoin your outward route. There's not really much virtue in this except to exercise the legs a bit and to enjoy a rather fine stand of mature forest.

Or you can take a short cut by following a muddy, rather slippery tractor track which heads downhill just as you reach the big tor. It leads you to a track which rejoins your upward route at the five-way junction.

If you need refreshment there are two pubs in Ashford — turn right when you get back to the roundabout.

25. Trooperstown Hill

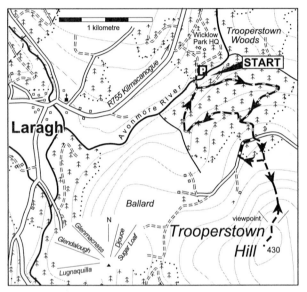

Distance: 6 km
Ascent: 250 m
Time: 2¼ hours
Equipment: OSI Discovery Sheet 56. Boots, weather gear.

For me this walk is full of nostalgia. The start is beside the Avonmore River, where you are very likely to see canoeists performing as I used to do, and nearly half of the walk is through Trooperstown Wood where I have spent many Sundays orienteering. In fact, I must confess that though I have often searched for orienteering controls on elusive boulders and re-entrants on the slopes of Trooperstown Hill (Maoilín, a little hill) I had never been to the summit until I climbed there to describe this walk. Essentially this is an up-and-back walk, but I've managed to introduce some variety by using different tracks. It is a good autumn or early winter walk for the autumn colours in the woods and the stark brown of the heather-covered hills.

From Dublin take the Wexford road (N11) to Kilmacanogue and turn right up the R755 towards Glendalough. About 2½ km beyond Annamoe there is a forest entrance on your left, signposted to the office of the Wicklow National Park. In the wood take the right fork (the left leads only to the Park Office) which brings you down to a car park beside the river — this is the start. You can also reach the forest entrance by the St Kevin's Glendalough bus — this will effectively add about 40 minutes onto your walking time because the bus is infrequent and your best bet on the way back will be to go to Laragh where there is a pub and a café where you can wait in comfort.

Cross the bridge, or if it takes your fancy, dance across the stepping stones. My guess is that until Coillte built the bridge, the stepping stones were part of a Mass Path for the people of Trooperstown to reach the church at Laragh. Linger on the bridge; even if there are no canoeists, the Avonmore is a fine, rocky, swirling stream.

At the T-junction beyond the bridge turn left (the right turn is for your return journey) and follow the good track through the forest, taking a right fork very soon. The track climbs easily through thick trees and then zigs back west. Here the trees have been felled and there is a fine view into Glendalough. Soon you turn left onto a surfaced road which takes you out of the woods to a T-junction with another tarred road. Immediately across this road is a rather rickety stile. Climb this carefully and follow a narrow track through young forest and gorse for a few minutes to another rickety stile which brings you onto the open heather slopes of Trooperstown Hill. There is a maze of tracks but you can hardly miss three parallel ones going up the hill, created, I suspect, by motorbikes. However, even these noisy things have their uses because the track on the right makes a pleasant route up the hill, pleasanter I confess than slogging through deep heather. Pause on the steep bit halfway up for the view — from the unmistakeable cone of the Great Sugar Loaf in the north-east round past Djouce (Walk 19), Glenmacnass, Glendasan to Derrybawn and Lugnaquilla itself. (This is the viewpoint on the map; it is better than the summit view which is restricted by the swell of the summit plateau.) Having admired, continue easily along the track to the summit cairn. Another view opens up to the east, a sea of rolling heather moor backed by the three rock tors of Carrick Mountain (Walk 24), struggling to appear above the conifer canopy.

For descent, follow your ascent route until the ground flattens out and then bear left along a good track which brings you out to the tarred road just beside a radio mast (this is a handy landmark). Turn right along the road past fields and a farm; in a couple of minutes mature forest appears on your left and then the tarred road you came up. Follow this as it swings first to the left (leaving your upward track on your right) and then back to the right through stands of fine mixed mature trees to the river, the bridge and the car park. Roundwood on your way back to Dublin offers a variety of pubs, cafés and restaurants. The same is true of Laragh in the other direction, and I have already suggested it for the bus users.

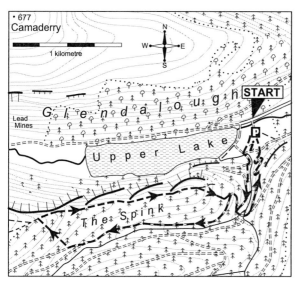

Distance: 5 km
Ascent: 320 m
Time: 2 hours
Equipment: OSI Discovery Sheet 56 or Harvey Map or National Park Trail map. Boots (trainers possible), weather gear, stick useful in descent.

This is the first of four walks in the Glendalough area and it may be objected that it is a couple too many, but since Glendalough (valley of the two lakes) *can probably claim to have the most beautiful scenery in Wicklow and has enormous historical interest, I have no compunction about including these walks, which are all very different in character. This first walk, the most dramatic of the four, has been designed to show off a superb view of the valley and its lakes which definitely can't be seen from a car. To see this view used to involve a struggle along the pitted, eroded crest of the Spink, but the National Park has built a sleeper track. You may object (as in principle I do) to such incursions of civilisation into wild country, but in this case I accept that a horrible walk has been*

Glendalough — The Spink

transformed for many less active walkers into a wonderful tour along this ridge high above the Upper Lake. I have described this walk so that you walk along the Spink facing east and can enjoy the view of the lakes without stopping or looking over your shoulder. It is also, I think, easier to walk up a steepish rough path and descend wooden steps than the other way round — but it's up to you! Spink by the way derives from the Irish Spinc, *meaning an overhanging cliff of rock, which is certainly what it looks like from below! The National Park have set out a number of way-marked walking trails, and this walk coincides with their blue trail. It is worth picking up their trail leaflet which shows several more trails that might interest you.*

The walk starts from the supervised car park (paying on Sundays) below the Upper Lake at Glendalough. By car take the N11 to Kilmacanogue, turn right onto the R755 to Laragh and beyond the bridge turn right along the R756, passing the Interpretive Centre and the Glendalough Hotel and continuing to the car park. By bus, take the St Kevin's bus (one of the few private buses still running in Ireland) which will take you as far as the Hotel. You must then walk a little over 1 km to the start (allow 15–20 minutes each way). Even with a car, if you have some spare time, you may like to start from the car park at the Interpretive Centre, the path beside the Lower Lake is very pleasant and there is an alternative path for return (Walk 27).

From the upper car park cross the grass, pass the small Information Centre and picking up the yellow man markers, cross the bridge and start up the forest road. Almost immediately the yellow man diverts you off the road onto steps up beside the stream. Soon you sight Poulanass Waterfall, and the Park has thoughtfully provided viewpoints for you to admire it. The path rejoins the road and you quickly come to a crossroads. Turn sharp right, waving farewell to a yellow man, and follow a forest road which soon swings left again (glimpses of the valley) and passes the foot of the steps which you will use on your descent from the Spink. Continue along the forest road, with views of the craggy wooded cirque at the head of the valley and after nearly 2 km reach a junction, where you bear right. Watch out now on your right for a break in the trees and a small cairn — it's only two minutes beyond the junction.

This is where you leave the road and climb quite steeply up a narrow path through the trees which brings you after a 200 m climb out onto the ridge of the Spink and the sleeper track. *(If you are coming from the other direction, the top of the path is not easy to find. From the dip in the ridge you climb some steps and then the track flattens out. Just before you come to the second set of steps you must look out for the path, not easily visible among the open trees. If you're lucky you'll see a yellow rag on a branch, but I can't promise it'll be there ...)*

Now head back east along the sleeper track with a wooded slope on your right and that precipitous cliff below you on the left. Don't worry though, the sleeper track is well away from the edge. As you walk, there are superb views down on the two lakes and the monastic settlement with its round tower. The last time I was up there it was a frosty, windless day under a cloudless blue sky and the reflections on the lakes of their tree-lined shores were perfect. The track dips and then rises again and at the top of the rise it is worth turning round to look *up* the valley. Beyond the Upper Lake are the ruins of the mining works and the tailings of the lead mines which flourished in the nineteenth century. The farthest workings were nicknamed Van Diemen's Land (now Tasmania), a penal colony to which many Irish convicts were transported. The level summit of the mountain behind isn't natural, it is the top of the Upper Reservoir of the Glendasan Pumped Storage Electricity Scheme.

Continuing the walk, the track turns right into the forest and descends by several hundred sleeper steps back to the forest road along which you set out. Turn left and retrace your outward route to the crossroads. Follow the yellow man across the bridge and then fork left onto a pleasant path which zigzags down on the opposite side of Poulanass to your outward route. At the bottom, turn left along the main track, and almost imediately, just before the Information Office turn right onto a tarmac path which leads straight to the car park. The Glendalough Hotel can offer food and drink and if you want mental sustenance as well, and haven't been there already, then you should certainly visit the Interpretive Centre and the 'Monastic City'.

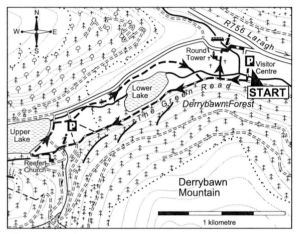

Distance: 3.8 km
Ascent: 50 m
Time: 1¼ hours
Equipment: OSI Discovery Sheet 56 or Harvey Map (National Park Trail map also useful). Trainers, rain gear.

This is a short easy walk on good paths in fabulous natural surroundings with a huge amount of historical interest. The trouble is of course that this makes it very popular, so don't go there on a sunny, summer, Sunday afternoon after a good lunch unless you really like crowds. We checked it out on a sunny, showery Sunday in mid-March and it was OK up to lunch time, but the Glendalough crowds were already building. I'd suggest a Saturday or weekday if you are free. The natural interest is that Glendalough (valley of the two lakes) is the most scenic of the Wicklow valleys, steep woods and crags framing a prospect from the Upper Lake to the heart of the mountains. The historical interest is the 'Monastic City' and the many other monastic sites which grew up around the original cell of St Kevin, hidden from the raiding Vikings, it was hoped, by its remote location. You park beside the fine Visitor Centre of the National Park where you can obtain a lot more information than I have space for here. The time I've given for the walk doesn't include for admiring either the view or the monastic buildings — perhaps two hours is a good total allocation! Part of this walk coincides with the National Park Green waymarked walk, but also with bits of the Grey walk and the Brown walk so it's best to ignore them all and stick to my description!

The road approach is as for Walk 26, but turn left into the National Park Visitor Centre Car Park just before the Glendalough Hotel. The car park is free, but watch the closing hours (5 pm in winter, later in summer). By bus, the St Kevin's bus will take you to the Hotel, and you can walk back the short distance to the Visitor Centre.

From the Centre, follow the arrows for the 'Monastic City' and the Wicklow Way yellow walking man signs across the river and turn right along the 'Green Road'. This is a delightful broad track along the south side of the valley, with the 'Monastic City' on your right and steep woods of oak, birch and conifer on your left. Soon you pass the Lower Lake, its reed beds glimpsed through the trees, and come out into the open with the Upper Lake and valley in view.

There are paths and arrows in all directions, and you can follow them where you choose, but I suggest you keep straight ahead past the useful Information Centre, past the bridge signposted Poulanass Waterfall (see Walk 26) and continue towards 'Reefert Church' and 'Site of St Kevin's original cell'. There's actually nothing there except a small, rather beautiful modern head of St Kevin by Imogen Stuart with the bird which allegedly nested on his outstretched hand, and a viewpoint high above the lake which offers fine views both up and down the valley. (This is not 'St Kevin's Bed', which is further up the lake shore and can only be reached by rough scrambling and climbing.) The path ends at the viewpoint, so retrace your steps (but going below Reefert Church) and turn left along a path which twists around and brings you to the open lake shore. The day I was checking, the wind was strong and the water level high, so that the breaking waves looked almost surfable and far up the lake the spray was blowing in the air. We passed a bench up to its knees in the water, but in spite of my urging, my wife wouldn't try to do better than King Canute.

The path leads you back to the main Upper Lake car park, generally buzzing with tourists, walkers, picnickers. Thread your way amongst the cars, and between the ladies' toilet and the café and past the bottle bank you will find a magnificent railed planked path. This takes you across the river and along between the road and the Lower Lake back towards your starting point. It is a delightful stretch of easy walking, winding along beside the Lake with the round tower and the tower of St Kevin's Church beckoning you on. Finally it twists to the south and goes back on stilts across the river to join the Green Road. You can follow your outward route back to the car park but I suggest that instead you recross the river, into the 'Monastic City'.

Spend as much or as little time as you like there and leave by the main entrance arch onto the main road, just near the Glendalough Hotel, and a great opportunity to relax over a drink or a meal. Here you can wait for the bus or go though the hotel car park, past the Visitor Centre to your car.

28. Between Glendalough and Laragh

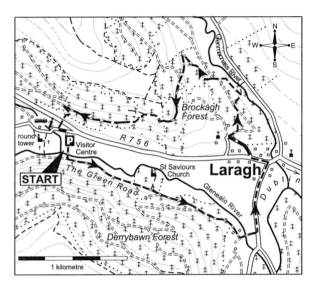

Distance: 6 km
Ascent: 150 m
Time: 2 hours
Equipment: OSI Discovery Sheet 56 or Harvey Map. Stout trainers and rain gear.

'Between Glendalough and Laragh' may conjure up for the Dubliner a narrow road with lots of cars, not the route you would want to walk at all. Well, you hardly touch the road in this exploration of the Glendalough Valley below the Visitor Centre. Instead you pass through an old deciduous wood on the south bank of the Glendasan River and so into the village of Laragh, with plenty of opportunities for refreshment. The return is along the Wicklow Way which rises above the valley and at its highest point has a superb view over the 'Monastic City' and the two lakes (to get good photographs it is best to reach the viewpoint fairly early in the day, before the sun shines straight down the valley in your eyes). The Centre suffers from the usual problem of Glendalough crowding, but

this beautiful walk does not seem to be very popular and when I last walked it with friends on the fine Sunday of a June bank holiday we met very few people.

For the approach from Dublin to the Glendalough Visitor Centre see Walk 26. If you come by car, the car park is free, but watch the closing hours (5 pm in winter, later in summer). If you come by St Kevin's bus, it will drop you at the Hotel, and the Visitor Centre is a very short walk back along the road. From the car park cross the river and turn left along the path through the woods beside the river. This is an old mixed wood, conifers mixed with beech, sycamore, oak and rowan, pleasant level walking. About 1 km along the path you will see a signpost directing you down to the left to St Saviour's Church, well worth the extra 10 or 20 minutes it will take to visit. A few minutes walk down to the river brings you to the church, a well-preserved ruin surrounded by a low bank in a clearing amongst tall conifers. It has an east window and a chancel arch with dog-tooth and other romanesque carving. Back on the route again, the brown markers of a National Park walk which have kept you company so far turn up the hill at the next junction, but you continue straight on.

Continue easily along the track to a big courtyard and building, once part of a mill, now a wool shop and hostel. Go through the arch and continue along the track, now surfaced, cross a humpback bridge over the Glendasan River and reach a public road. I am afraid there is no alternative to this road, which tends to be rather busy at weekends, so turn left, keep to the far side, face the traffic and walk circumspectly for the 0.6 kilometre to Laragh village. You can slake your thirst or calm your nerves in one of several establishments here!

Turn left at the T-junction, and then just before a petrol station turn right up a narrow road, which soon leads you to a parking area just opposite the Catholic church. Turn right here along a forest road. A very short distance along it, just before two huts, one on either side of the road, a narrow path leads into the woods on the left. Although the forest road would eventually bring you to your route, the path, if you spot it, is both shorter and much pleasanter. It brings you out on the same road, having cut off a large loop, just before a path crosses the road. Turn right along the path which leads to a junction with the Wicklow Way just near a bridge over the

Glenmacnass River. It is worth diverting down to the bridge to look at the river, here tumbling amongst rocks, before following the signs for the Way towards Glendalough. A narrow path winds through the trees above the river and then bears left to rejoin the forest road (leaving the road was an unnecessary diversion, a little longer this time, but to my mind making a change from the forest roads which form most of the rest of the walk). You are now walking through the property of Coillte, the semi-state company which manages most of the Republic's plantations. Its remit is to make money by growing and felling trees but it does show an interest in the requirements of walkers with the paths, markers, and bridges which you meet here.

From now on simply follow the little yellow men markers. These lead you easily uphill in a big zigzag through fine mature pine trees which I hope won't have been felled when you make this walk. As you turn the first V-bend, you can see open pastures on your right; notice the piles of rock scattered around which have been laboriously cleared to make good pasture out of a stony hillside. When last I passed, gorse had taken root amongst the rock piles and the yellow blossoms amongst the rocks were a striking sight.

Fork left following the arrows at the next bend and follow a pleasant, slightly descending forest road amongst mature trees (though marks on the trees foretell they may soon be for felling). The road bears to the right and there's a gate and stile into a com-pletely contrasting area. A narrow, rocky track climbs steeply up through high gorse, but don't complain because it soon levels out, the gorse is only chest high and there is a sudden and quite unex-pected view of the Glendalough Valley, the 'Monastic City', the Lower Lake and the Upper Lake squeezed between steep-sided wooded ridges. The ridge on the left (south) is followed by Walk 26. When you have sufficiently admired and photographed, continue down the steep, narrow track which passes through a high wicket gate onto a now-welcome level forest road.

Follow the road through mature forest sloping steeply down on your left, whence you can hear the hum of traffic on the Glendalough Road and get the occasional glimpse of a house. After some 500 m a marker directs you left diagonally down to the foot of the forest. Here you find what must be one of the greatest collection of stiles along any walking route — five in the space of about 50 m

— to get you out of Coillte property, across the track between two pastures, into National Park property and down to the public road to the Wicklow Gap.

Cross the road and follow a track down to the Glendalough Hotel. Turn left to return to the car park, or keep straight ahead into the bar!

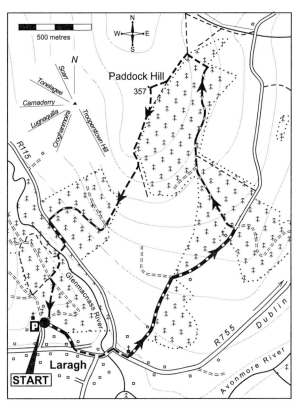

Distance: 5.7 km
Ascent: 210 m
Time: 2 hours (1½ hours if you go straight up and back)
Equipment: OSI Discovery Sheet 56 or Harvey or Healy Maps. Boots (trainers possible), rain gear, stick useful on descent.

The fourth of a group of walks based on Laragh/Glendalough, and likely to be the least crowded. Paddock Hill is more the top of a spur than a real hill on its own, but it offers some pleasant walking, a delightful open ridge and good views to Lugnaquilla and the hills round to Scarr. I have made a circular walk by approaching it along the back road towards Oldbridge, climbing up through a forest and emerging suddenly onto the high open hill. With the thrutch over, you can appreciate Paddock Hill itself and dawdle down along the Wicklow Way to Glenmacnass and so back to the start. You can, of course, go up the descent route and down the same way and save some time. The walk is as easily done from the St Kevin's bus as it is by car.

Drive or bus to Laragh as described in Walk 26. If by car, in Laragh turn right after the bridge and turn right again up the narrow road just before the shop and petrol pumps and park in the open space near the church (the bus leaves you at the bottom of this road).

Start the walk by retracing your approach back across the bridge and a short way along the Dublin Road (busy, but there is a footpath) to a road on the left signposted to St John's Protestant Church. Follow this road which climbs past the church and a number of houses. It is a quiet road and when I checked out this walk I only met two cars in the 20 minutes I spent walking it. However, there is one disadvantage; every house seems to have at least one, if not two dogs, which break into a frenzy of barking as you pass. A forest appears on your left and soon you reach two forest entrances opposite each other. Enter the left one and follow the forest road (not marked on Sheet 56) which diagonals up the hill. Felling was going on when I walked the route, so it may have been replanted when you walk it. The forest road will be there anyway and for much of the walk there are fields below and to your right views across to the east. When the forest road finishes at a turning circle, continue for a few metres into standing native trees and turn left up a narrow path near an earth bank. Soon there is open hillside ahead beyond an easily crossed fence. Beyond the fence is a track which you follow to the left and to a yellow man welcoming you to the Wicklow Way.

Follow the Way south, rising gently, and where it levels out (beyond a small pool), leave it and climb to the right onto the top of the ridge. This is more or less level and you can take your choice as to the exact position of the 'summit'. I picked a group of rocks which provided a seat from which to admire the view and eat some chocolate. I was there on a cold, sunny winter's day in the late afternoon without a breath of wind and no one else in sight. I have seldom felt so happy and relaxed on a mountain top. To the south the whole range from Croaghanmoira (Walk 32) was spread out, with Lug itself well covered with snow. Round to the north-west the broad ridge, speckled with the occasional boulder, led up to the snow-dusted ridge of Scarr (Walk 20), its summit obscured by a cloud.

Return to the Wicklow Way and follow it down across the open hillside to a stile into a young birch wood. (Many of the woods round here will be handed over by Coillte to the National Park, so broadleaved are favoured.) The path joins a forest road which curls round to bring you into Glenmacnass (*Gleann Log an Easa*) and a public road. Go left along the road for about 200 m and turn right at the signpost down a path to the fine wooden bridge over the Glenmacnass River. Beyond the bridge, you fork left to leave the Wicklow Way (signposts) and follow a broad track through the woods until you meet a forest road. Turn left and after 100 m or so pick up a path through the woods on the right which cuts off a long dog-leg of the forest road and brings you out just near your car. If you came by bus, when you reach the open area, go left down the road which brings to the main road in a couple of minutes. *If you are going up Paddock Hill by this route, the shortcut path is 100 m from the car parking area just before two huts, one on either side of the forest road.*

Laragh village has two churches, a pub and a café — what more can you want?

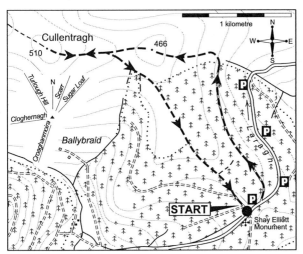

Distance: 5½ km
Ascent: 220 m
Time: 2 hours
Equipment: OSI Discovery Sheet 56 or Harvey or Healy Maps. Boots, weather gear.

Cullentragh is the nearest mountain to the Military Road on the ridge between Glendalough and Glenmalure, really handy for a short walk. Most people seem to go straight up and back but with the aid of the Harvey and Healy Maps, whose larger scale enables them to show paths not marked on the Discovery map, I have found a circular route which also takes in another summit. Although the car journey to the start takes a little longer than the ascent (allow 5 hours door to door from the centre of Dublin) it is a worthwhile walk which gets you very pleasantly and gently to a rounded summit with views stretching from the Great Sugar Loaf to Lugnaquilla. Most of it is on tracks, and at the time of writing most of the rest was easy walking on recently burnt heather.

Take the N11 to Kilmacanogue, turn right onto the R755 to Laragh and continue on the R755 towards Rathdrum for about 1.5 km. Turn right up a narrow road, the Military Road, signposted to Glenmalure and follow it as it meanders up to the top of the ridge between Glendalough and Glenmalure. Just over the crest is a monument to the cyclist Shay Elliott. Park there. (Shay was a racing cyclist of the late fifties and early sixties, famed for being the first Irishman to wear the yellow shirt on the *Tour de France*. The monument here overlooks one of his favourite training areas.) Park at the forest entrance. When we hear so much about access problems it is pleasing to see the notice erected by the Wicklow Uplands Council welcoming walkers to Glenmalure.

Don't go straight into the forest; walk back up the road for a few minutes to another forest entrance and follow the track, rather muddy, heading north and, I am sorry to say, descending a little. However, it is only 15 minutes or so to the edge of the forest and better things. Cross the very battered fence and head diagonally up the hill. In May, when I last walked it, the bracken was only beginning to sprout, but it may be harder going in high summer. Again this section doesn't last long and in a few minutes you meet an old track. Follow it uphill until it veers off to the left when you should continue straight up the hill over heather and grass with small rocks and many lumps of white quartz. Somewhere underneath your feet is the granite batholith which was pushed up in the Caledonian mountain building 450 million years ago. A skin of schist overlies the summit of this as of many Wicklow mountains; the quartz probably indicates the granite isn't too far below you.

There follows a head-down plod up the hillside, but suddenly you come onto the rounded summit, lift your head and a wide new view appears. A slight dip, and a broad ridge leads towards Cullentragh itself, backed by Mullacor and the edge of the Glendalough forest, while beside you is a fine cairn. You are standing on the roundel contour on Sheet 56, to which Harvey has added the spot height 466.

Descend the gentle slope to the saddle and start up the slope towards Cullentragh. It gets rougher and tussocky as you climb and you may prefer to veer left off the ridge onto the track which is visible beside an old wire fence. If you are using the Harvey Map, you are probably bracing yourself for a 170 m climb to the 610 spot height, but don't worry, that is a mistake for 510 as Sheet 56 can show you. It is a very gentle climb and after crossing a stile it lands you easily on the vague, rounded, cairnless summit of Cullentragh.

The view is magnificent. Apart from the sector blocked by the bulk of Mullacor you have a 360° sweep. Clockwise your eye swings from the reservoir on Camaderry over Tonelagee, Scarr, Djouce and the distant, but always recognisable, Great Sugar Loaf round over Kirikee to Croaghanmoira's perfect cone (Walk 32) and across Glenmalure to Carrawaystick and Cloghernagh. Now walk a little north and the view opens up below you to the jagged ridge of Derrybawn backed by the woods on both sides of Glendalough. If using Sheet 56 you will note that this time it is OSI which has slipped up — none of the trees on this side of Glendalough are marked!

On Cullentragh I feel a wonderful sense of being truly embraced by the Wicklow Mountains. You are high enough to have valleys and habitations to overlook, and yet you are surrounded by higher hills, and while it is the fashion to condemn the forests creeping up the hillsides, their sombre green creates a strong contrast with the paler tones of heather and grass, and, if you pick the right day, blue sky and white cloud complete a superb mountain picture.

Enough chatter. Go back along the path by which you probably finished the ascent, follow it, passing below the summit of 466 and into young woodland. The path is visible straight ahead, and looks to rise again seriously but like all the climbs on this walk it is easier than it looks — the rise is a mere 20 m! Descend straight ahead into mature forest, and ignoring two roads branching off to the right, continue on to meet the public road and your car.

For refreshment, I recommend that you continue down into Glenmalure (it is about 3 km) to the Glenmalure Lodge Hotel which always welcomes walkers and climbers.

Note: By the time you read this the mapmakers may have corrected their mistakes!

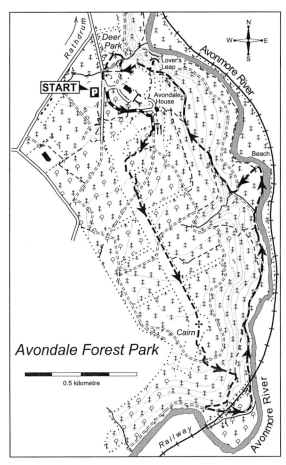

Distance: 4½ km
Ascent: 80 m
Time: 1½ hours plus lots of viewing time
Equipment: OSI Discovery Sheet 62, Avondale Map Guide. Good walking shoes, rain gear, tree and flower books.

As most Irish people know, Avondale House, built in 1777, was the birthplace and home of Charles Stewart Parnell, one of the great leaders of the struggle for Irish freedom. In 1904 the Estate was bought by the State, which used it for experimental forest plots for a variety of species. (You can see these plots on either side flanking the Great Ride.) The house was used as a training centre for foresters. It was retained by the Forestry Division of the new State which continued to use the house for training courses. In 1984 it was handed over to Coillte, who have since restored the house as the historic home of Parnell. The house is open from 17 March to 31 October from 11 am to 6 pm (ring Avondale House +353–404–456111 to check times). The name comes from the nearby river, the Avonmore (Aibhainn Mhor, big river).

I have tried to show the exact route of my suggested walk on the sketch map opposite, but I recommend you buy the map and guide available at the gate or the house. It is on a much larger scale and has much more information than I can fit in, especially about the various exotic trees to be found. This map has a number of recommended trails, and I have used what I think are the best bits of all of them in my walk. The 1½ hours I have allowed is just for walking. When we checked this for the book we took 3 hours to walk round, there are so many interesting trees and views to examine and admire. The whole Forest Park reflects great credit on Coillte.

We checked it in April, when the spring flowers (celandine, buttercups, violets, wood sorrel) were out, anxious to bloom before the tree cover blocked the sun, but I think Avondale is a delightful place to visit at nearly any time of year.

Take the N11 (Wexford road) out of Dublin to Rathnew, go right at the roundabout and where the N11 swings left under a railway bridge keep straight on along the R752 signposted Rathdrum. When you approach Rathdrum do not go straight up the hill into the village but bear left and continue to a crossroads. Turn left there and after about 2 km the entrance to Avondale lies straight ahead. Drive into the car park (sometimes there's a charge, sometimes not!). It is possible to get the train to Rathdrum and walk — this adds a good half-hour each way to the walk. Check the train times!

From the car park follow the signs to Avondale House and there pick up the red arrows of the Exotic Tree Trail which lead you to the wide Great Ride stretching down to the south-east between fine mature woodlands, with many superb old trees. When the Exotic Tree Trail turns left, continue down the Great Ride into a dip and then rise up to a large cairn. It looks exciting — a beehive hut perhaps, but it is only a heap of large stones. However, what is exciting is the view from the cairn south across the Avonmore River to Croaghan Kinsella, last outlier of the Wicklow Mountains on the border with Co. Wexford.

Continue for a little down the Great Ride and then turn left into the wood, following the white arrows of the River Walk and the orange arrows of the Cairn Walk. At a junction keep straight on following the River Walk. This descends quite steeply (though not as steeply as the 'Danger — Steep Slope' sign might lead you to expect) to a T-junction. Turn right and follow the track to another T-junction where you turn left and go under the railway. The track swings round left, beside a millrace and then, crossing beneath the railway again, follows the bank of the Avonmore. The walk gives good views of the river which is here shallow and rocky — you might see a canoeist playing in the rapids.

Soon you meet the Exotic Tree Trail again and at the junction is a silver fir which was planted by the builder of Avondale House, Samuel Hayes, more than two centuries ago. Keeping along the River Walk you can admire on your left the red bark of the western red cedars, which look tall enough though they are only half the height to which they grow in their native American forests. Here too are sequoias, dramatically large here, but mere infants compared with their 2,000-year-old brothers in California. The track veers away from the river beside a streamlet but you turn right along a narrow path (white arrow) which crosses the streamlet and follows the river to 'The Beach', a sandy stretch where the river broadens into a wide still pool. There's a bench beside another danger notice relating to a bank nearly half a metre high, and if you don't fall over it, it's a nice picnic spot. (I should mention that there are benches scattered throughout the woods.) Suitably re-energised, leave the River Walk and turn left along a broad path which takes you to a double junction where you pick up the Exotics again, turning right and climbing gently up the hill. You pass a couple of 'Monkey Puzzle' pine (*araucaria* from Chile) and then come to a path on the left (red arrow) heading towards the house. But at the next junction, you turn right onto the Pine Tree Trail (blue arrows) passing below a massive stone wall which was probably an eighteenth-century 'Folly', and a fine Japanese cedar before reaching an open glade, a wider track on your right and an arrow to Lover's Leap. The Leap itself is not wildly dramatic but its 'Danger — Steep Slope' sign is this time somewhat of an understatement. We amused ourselves concocting other signs that might be suitable 'Leaps by non-lovers strictly forbidden' or 'Book early — only one performance per generation'. The view is marred by a large pine, but that does at least block out the sight of a recently re-opened and very noisy quarry (we were there on a weekday).

Returning from the Leap, turn right along the track until you meet a crossroads. Turn right, following a white arrow in reverse, cross a small stream and immediately turn left along a path which brings you to the deer enclosure. The first time I was there a fine red-deer stag was in residence. The next time there was an inquisitive family of, I think, red-sika crosses. Sika deer from Japan were imported in the nineteenth century for the Powerscourt Estate. Some escaped and interbred with native reds. Leaving the enclosure by a path at 90° to your arrival path will bring you onto the entrance road. Follow this to the front of Avondale House, a typical eighteenth-century gentleman's house, which you should certainly visit if you have time. Beside the house you will find a pleasant restaurant in which to relax. A little further on is a children's playground, but on the way stop to admire a super supercilious owl, carved in wood, looking at his toes peeking out and clearly thinking all these humans are pretty stupid. At the playground, carved by the same artist, is a totem pole; a fox chases a squirrel up a tree, another squirrel looks on, a bird roosts peacefully above them. As you return to your car, or set out on your walk to the station, you pass two more wood sculptures, a forester and a walker, but neither of them are as effective as the owl or the totem pole.

If you really need alcohol, there's a sufficiency of pubs in Rathdrum.

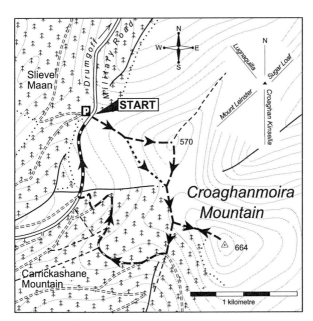

Distance: 5 km
Ascent: 300 m
Time: 2–2¼ hours
Equipment: OSI Discovery Sheet 62 or Healy Map (Sheet 56 useful for view and road approach). Boots, sticks, weather gear.

Driving into the hills from Dublin we almost always turn off the N11 at Kilmacanogue and climb up the winding hill beside the Great Sugar Loaf until the road suddenly flattens out on Callary Bog, and straight ahead in the distance there appears a perfectly pyramidal summit, Croaghanmoira (Cruachan maoir, *the mountain of the steward*). *As we drive south it disappears and comes back into view several times, always maintaining the same symmetrical appearance. Close up, when you are ready to climb it, the perfect pyramidal form is still there — though the angle looks a lot steeper. It is over 50 years since I first climbed it, and I still find it a very attractive short walk. A warning: the forest roads are not marked accurately on Sheet 62 — the Healy Map is correct, and so is the sketch map on the previous page!*

Drive from Dublin as for Walk 30 but continue down into Glenmalure. At the crossroads continue straight on along the Military Road, passing the bleak high ruin of the Glenmalure Barracks, one of those built by the British in the aftermath of the 1798 Rising. While the main rising was quickly put down, fighting continued in the Wicklow Mountains for several years and the Military Road with this and several other fortified barracks were built to tame the area. The road winds up the valley southward for about 4 km to the top of the pass leading to the Aghavannagh Valley. Exactly at the top a forest road leads off to the right and beside it lies a big granite boulder with a red cross on it (I can't promise the boulder will still be there when you visit). Anyway, boulder or no boulder there is plenty of space to park.

Now Croaghanmoira stands up between Pt 570 (no height on OSI map) on the left and a big plantation on the right. Go through a gate on the left of the road and mount easily up a broad rough track which is heading for Pt 570. However, it bears away to the right and you will have to leave it and climb straight up over rough heathery slopes to the summit. It is an airy point and I ate my lunch in a hollow looking at the view and listening to the skylarks. The view is much the same as from Croaghanmoira so I won't describe it here. On the summit you meet a rough track which you can follow to the right, descending gently (bilberry feast here in July) to the corner of the wood. (If you don't want to climb Pt 570, stay on the track you started on which rejoins the route at this corner.)

Turn left onto a good track which leads you gently upward beside the forest to a bend in the forest boundary and the junction with a forest track (the track you will take on the descent). But on the ascent continue up the track beside the forest which steepens considerably and climbs straight up for what looks an interminable distance to a fence post on the ridge. Just plod on and you will find the distance isn't so far; when you reach the ridge the good track swings right but you keep to a rough track which continues upward and in a minute or two you are at the trig pillar.

Like so many outlying summits Croaghanmoira is a fine viewpoint, all of 360°. Far away a little east of north is the easily-recognised pyramidal Great Sugar Loaf and moving counter-clockwise the whole Wicklow chain can be seen, with Lugnaquilla just appearing over the nearer Carrawaystick Mountain. To the south-west beyond the Aghavannagh Valley the Wicklow hills gradually reduce in height and then rise up again proudly to Mount Leinster. Swinging east of south is the isolated Croaghan Kinsella on the Wexford border and then glimpses of the coast northward and back to the Great Sugar Loaf.

For the descent, retrace your steps to the bend in the forest and turn left down a forest track to a T-junction. Turn right along a track which rises gently over a spur and then drops equally gently through mature conifers. It is said that these coniferous woods don't have much bird life, but on the June day when I last walked through this wood, there was a whole orchestra of birdsong. Ignore two tracks leading down to the left, one on each side of the spur, but soon after the track has taken a sharp turn towards the south, turn right along a narrower muddy track which brings you in a few minutes out onto the road at the corner of the forest. Turn right and 10 minutes walk will bring you back to your car.

On the way home I strongly recommend a visit to the Glenmalure Lodge Hotel, in whose bar walkers will find a warm welcome.

33. Glenmalure — O'Dwyer's Rock

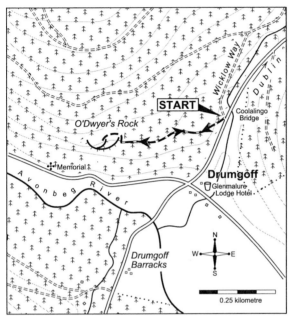

Distance: 2 km
Ascent: 40 m
Time: 40 minutes
Equipment: OSI Discovery Sheet 56, (preferable) Harvey Map. Walking shoes or trainers, rain gear.

Do I expect you to drive all the way to Glenmalure just for a 40-minute walk? Well, hardly, but really Glenmalure itself is such a wonderful remote valley that it would be worth a visit even without a walk. I can't claim it is as beautiful as Glendalough (it has no lakes for one thing), but it has far fewer visitors. Since the only longer walk in the valley is the hardest in the book and unsuitable for families, I have included two short walks, this one which has a great view down lower Glenmalure as well as Walk 34 which has an even more stunning view of the upper valley.

Glenmalure — O'Dwyer's Rock

*In fact you could, as I did, do both in one day. It doesn't seem crowded — I was last there on a fine July Sunday and only met two people, when there were traffic jams at Laragh. **Please do not do this walk between the beginning of April and the end of June — a peregrine nests here sometimes.***

Michael O'Dwyer, as every Irish person knows, was one of the leaders of the 1798 revolt in Wicklow. He escaped capture but eventually gave himself up and was transported to Australia, where he became a respected citizen and eventually a sergeant of the police. Anyway it is alleged that he used this rock as a viewpoint from which to watch the activities at the Drumgoff Barracks, one the several barracks on the Military Road, built after 1798 to subdue the rebels hiding in the hills.

Drive from Dublin to Glenmalure as described in Walk 30 but continue towards Glenmalure and park just before the Drumgoff crossroads at the forest entrance just over Coolalingo Bridge (there's a Wicklow Way marker and signpost). Take the forest road on the left (not the Wicklow Way). Rising gently it passes between fenced-off areas where it is good to see that broad-leaf trees have been planted, and then levels out in mature forest, which is part planted conifers, and part mature oaks. The road stops as you emerge into the open, opposite the lower portion of the Rock. A footpath climbs up the open hillside and brings you to the top of the Rock. This is open (perhaps it was different two centuries ago) and offers a fine broad view of the green meadows of lower Glenmalure, framed between Carriglineen on the left and Fananeirin on the south. Directly below is the Barracks. I did not go directly to the top of the Rock but climbed halfway up the path and traversed to a wooded platform on the Rock. Hidden among the trees I had a perfect view, as O'Dwyer might have had, of the Barracks and Drumgoff Bridge, and so warning of any search party setting out. Perhaps he saw the soldiers drilling in front of the Barracks — I saw half-a-dozen holiday caravans!

From the map it looked simple to climb up to the forest road above and so make a circular walk. I did it, but it was not simple — very steep, with no path and broken branches to climb over. Much better to return the way you came!

As you will have seen from the Rock, the Glenmalure Lodge

Hotel is only a couple of minutes from Coolalingo Bridge — turn left at the crossroads.

If you turn right at the cross roads, just a short distance up there is a big boulder with an inscription to O'Dwyer and Fiach MacHugh O Broin.

While we are on history, one school of thought maintains that Art O'Neill, the Ulster chief who escaped in January 1592 from Dublin Castle with Red Hugh O'Donnell, walked down the east side of the Wicklow hills and died under an overhanging rock near the high point of the Military Road coming into Glenmalure. There is a cairn of white quartz stones '300 yards south of it' (I haven't found it) which the local people maintain is Art O'Neill's grave.

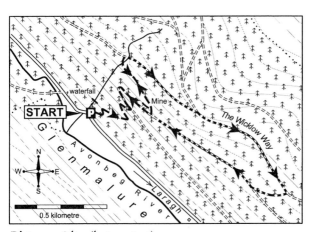

Distance: 2 km (but see text)
Ascent: 180 m
Time: 1 hour
Equipment: OSI Discovery Sheet 56 or Harvey Map. Trainers, walking shoes or boots, rain gear, sticks useful.

I've already sung the praises of Glenmalure in the Introduction to Walk 33, but you may still think that a walk to the very dull hole that used to be a mine is hardly worth the journey. But ... I've walked this route twice recently, the first time, by chance on my way to somewhere else, and when my companion insisted I had to include it in this book somehow, I walked it again, and decided, yes it is worth including! It offers really fine views of the head of Glenmalure without too much climbing and while the mine is simply a hole in the hillside, the approach is an old track through the woods, not a modern forest road. The start itself is worth a visit. There's a car park, some picnic tables and a delightful waterfall as background — take granny to mind the baby while you nip off for a short walk. Of course there is a problem — it's popular. So don't go there on a summer Sunday afternoon if you like a bit of quiet. I arrived there on the June bank-holiday Monday at noon, and it was

Glenmalure — an Old Mine

deserted. When I arrived back one-and-a-half hours later there were 4 families there, but even so it didn't feel too crowded.

Drive to Glenmalure as for Walk 33 but turn right up the valley at the Drumgoff crossroads. Nearly 3 km up the valley the road crosses the middle of a wide slope of sand and stones. Almost immediately after this watch for a track on the right which brings you to car parking in a few metres. It is marked as a car park on both maps, but it is only obvious when you've passed it!

From the flat ground in front of the waterfall, go right, crossing the stream by the remains of a culvert (three concrete pipes). A path, the old track to the mine, brings you easily uphill, zigzagging under an arch of trees. After a few minutes you emerge onto open hillside, above the slope of sand and stones you crossed down below in the car. There is a sharp bend here, with an old stone retaining wall, the first obvious sign of the reason for the path's existence — it had to be a good path to bring down ore, probably on asses. Another sharp bend and then the path emerges onto a forest road. Memorise the spot, because you will be returning that way, and the point where the path leaves the forest road is not obvious.

Turn left up the forest road. This where I had a bit of excitement which I have to tell you about, even though it must be astronomically unlikely that you'll be as lucky. In the middle of the road I noticed a lump of dung, nearly as large as a golf ball which seemed to be moving. I looked closer; it was moving. I looked even closer and, almost underneath the dung, pushing hard, was a beetle about half an inch long. Movement was slow and obviously very hard work as the beetle pushed one side, then the other and finally disappeared underneath. I walked on a few paces and there was another moving lump of dung. This time I got my camera out and was trying to photograph the action when four walkers appeared, wondering what I was at; I explained and they stared also. Neither they nor I had ever seen the like before. Then suddenly the beetle, shrugged its shoulders, as it were, and beetled off. It was around one o'clock — perhaps it was lunch-time?

I followed the forest road round a V-bend and still climbing, passed below a mound of sand and small stones, tailings from the mine. I looked to see whether there were any fragments of ore, but found none; lots of shiny bits, but they were all mica from the schist rock. I can't find any records of this mine; judging by the size of the tailings heap it wasn't worked for long. I presume that they were mining lead like the larger and better known mines in Glendalough. Like them, the lead would have been brought for smelting to Ballycorus.

A little further, just before another area of stones and sand (but natural this time, I think), a narrow path leads coyly up to the left. Not easy to see, but its location between the heaps makes it recognisable. Ten or twenty metres up this path, there's big overgrown depression below you — the mine. There's nothing to see and I've really dragged you up here on false pretences, but just go a little further, out into the open hillside, with only some mountain ash saplings growing amidst the undergrowth and you have a super panoramic view of the head of Glenmalure. On the left is the steep edge of the Cloghernagh plateau, next to the Baravore cliffs on the west side of the Fraughan Rock Glen, then Benleagh hiding Camenabologue. To its right the Table Track is visible, which crosses the gap at the head of the valley to lead to the Glen of Imaal. Finally the rounded top of Conavalla completes the view.

This is the minimum, but having come so far, you might like to explore where the path will take you. This is where boots are preferable, because a stream has taken over the path for some distance, and even when dry it is fairly rough. A narrow path, it winds in among the gorse bushes across open hillside with undergrowth and young broadleaves, so you don't lose the view as you climb higher. The path debouches onto a wide forest road where there is a wide view up Glenmalure and additionally north-west towards Lugduff.

I think this is a worthwhile little extension which only adds 15–20 minutes to your time if you return down the way you came up. It is also possible to return by going right (east) along the forest road and turning right whenever you get the chance which will bring you back past the tailings mound at the cost of a rather dull walk and an extra 3 km walk which might take you an extra ¾ of an hour.

Rehydration, as for all these Glenmalure walks, is at the Glenmalure Lodge Hotel at the Drumgoff crossroads.

Glenmalure — an Old Mine

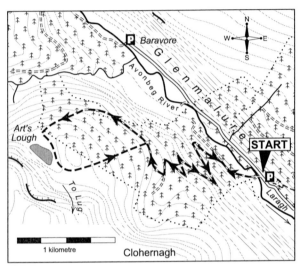

Distance: 7½ km
Ascent: 350 m
Time: 3 hours
Equipment: OSI Discovery Sheet 56 or (preferable) Harvey Map. Boots, weather gear, sticks, compass if the cloud is down.

This is quite a serious route, not exceptionally long, but in parts it is quite rough, and it is also boggy, so it is really best as a summer walk. If you own a pair of gaiters then bring them to keep your trousers dry. You are rewarded for your efforts by reaching a really remote-seeming lake — you can't see down to a valley at all. There is another good reason for this walk. This guidebook is suitable for inexperienced walkers, but some of them will certainly want to go on to do longer and harder walks. Especially when finding the way is at all difficult, I've gone into a lot of detail, something which you won't find in guidebooks for the longer walks. To walk safely over the bigger Wicklow hills you need more than an ability to read a guidebook — you need to be able to read a map, use a compass, and have some idea of route finding, in other words to be able

116

to navigate. You need these for the time when the weather closes in or when a member of your party is tired or ill. Also, I haven't included many walks with the unavoidable ingredient of most Wicklow walks — lots of bog. So here is a walk where I can hardly do more than suggest the route from the end of the forest road to the lough and where bogland is definitely an ingredient.

Another reason for its inclusion is that if you've graduated from my easy walks to something longer, then it is the start of a very good way up Lugnaquilla, about which I've included a short note.

Drive up Glenmalure as for Walk 34. You can park as for Walk 34 or drive on a 100 m or so and park at the forest entrance on the left, which is the start of the walk. Follow the forest road over the bridge and past some newly-planted oak and beech saplings. When we were there, sadly, a sizeable number of cattle had got among the trees, and many of the trees were lying over drunkenly, their protective sheaths scattered — this obviously wasn't the first invasion. The road begins to climb, and you take the left fork at a junction. It continues to rise through half-grown spruce trees, the monotony broken by the road crossing mossy waterfalls, and in May, when we were there, by the bright green young shoots on the spruce. Be grateful also for the steady, easy gain in height. After five V-bends the road flattens at the mouth of the amphitheatre below the Bendoo cliffs. Turn right here onto a road (not marked on Sheet 56) which contours the hill, rising gently. You soon pass a broad ride climbing the hill on your left — this is your descent route.

The road deteriorates to a track and then to a path. It emerges onto open ground and more or less disappears, but look to your left and there is a gap in a band of trees. Go through this and you will find a narrow boggy path between a bank on your left, and the trees on your right (you may prefer to climb the bank and walk through heather parallel to the bank and trees). Follow the trees to a kink in the bank, where the route leaves them and slants up the hillside on a vague path over heather and bog. Soon a wire fence (not on either map) comes into view, and when you see a stile, cross it. Walk the boggy path beside the fence, with Art's Lough now visible on your right. Climb over a cross fence, and follow vague paths to two large recumbent grey boulders, which are an excellent dry place for a rest and lunch.

You can really imagine you are in a wilderness. Facing south across the Lough you see the steep rocky slopes of Clohernagh, Lugnaquilla's eastern outlier. On your left a ramp leads up towards Clohernagh — that's the way to 'Lug', but not for today! On your right, framed in the outlet from the Lough, are the Baravore cliffs above the unseen Fraughan Rock Glen, behind you a heathery bump hides Glenmalure and your route up — bar a battered fence, there are no signs of human life.

Relaxed and rested, now for the return. Walk east, between the fence on your left and the ramp on your right, picking a route through the heather and bog. Keep an eye on the fence, and when you see the second stile beyond the boulders, cross it. There is a kink in the fence just beyond the stile (this where the fence starts on Harvey, though it is not on Sheet 56 at all) and almost immediately the broad ride down through the trees becomes obvious. There is a path, very pleasant on grass for a change, which descends steeply down the ride. You pass a heap of planks and poles; I remember when this was a lookout point until a gale blew it down. Continue on down, the path getting rather muddier and wetter, until you meet the forest road and your upward route. Reverse it back to your car.

On your way back, I suggest a visit to the Glenmalure Lodge Hotel, just near the crossroads.

A brief note on climbing Lugnaquilla. From the two boulders climb the ramp and bear right up steeper slopes to the summit of Clohernagh. From that summit a path along a broad ridge, firm ground underfoot, and a final easy climb overlooking the cliff of the South Prison will bring you to the big summit cairn of Lugnaquilla, (*Log-na-gcoilleach,* the hollow of the cocks) the highest mountain in Leinster at 925 m. On the return, be careful to pick the correct ridge, it is quite easy to veer to the right onto the ridge leading to Corrigasleggaun. The round trip will take about 6 hours.

Bibliography

There are a number of books which will enhance your enjoyment of these walks. The most important are:

Conlin, Stephen and de Courcy, John, *Anna Liffey*, Dublin 1988.
Delany, Ruth, *The Grand Canal*, Dublin 1995.
Delany, Ruth, *The Royal Canal*, Dublin 1992.
Fewer, Michael, *By Swerve of Shore*, Dublin 1998.
Harbison, Peter, *National Monuments of Ireland*, Dublin 1992.
Healy, Elizabeth (ed.), *The Book of the Liffey*, Dublin 1988.
Hutchinson, Clive, *Birds of Dublin and Wicklow*, Dublin 1975.
Jeffrey, D.W. (ed.), *North Bull Island*, Dublin 1977.
Joyce, Weston St J., *The Neighbourhood of Dublin*, reprinted, Dublin 1971 (although first published in 1912 it is still an interesting source of historical information, and an index to the enormous changes in Dublin during the twentieth century).
Ó Maitiú, Séamas and O'Reilly, Barry, *Ballyknockan*, Dublin 1997.
Price, Liam, *The Placenames of Co. Wicklow*, several vols Dublin 1945– (this fascinating series is the source of most of my place-name information).
The Flora of County Dublin, Dublin Field Naturalists Club, Dublin 1998.
The Open Forest, Coillte, Dublin n.d.
The Parks of Fingal, Fingal County Council n.d.

For more short walks near Dublin try *Easy Walks near Dublin*, Joss Lynam, Dublin 1999.

If you want longer walks near Dublin, Wicklow and the southeast, try *Walk Guide East of Ireland*, Jean Boydell, David Herman, Miriam Joyce McCarthy, 3rd Ed., Dublin 1999.

If the waterside takes your fancy, *Irish Waterside Walks*, Michael Fewer, Dublin 1997, describes such walks all round the country, including some around Dublin which aren't in this book.

Wicklow Way Map Guide, EastWest Mapping, Wexford 2003 is one of several guides to the Way, which can be taken in short sections.

Harbison, Peter and Lynam, Joss, *St Kevin's Way*, Dublin 2002 — there is a lot on road, but you can pick interesting off-road sections.

You will also find ideas for walks around Dublin in the books of David Herman, Christopher Moriarty and Pat Liddy.